F.M.L.

Standing Out &
Leading Others

Dedication

To Christina, without you we wouldn't be around. Thank you for your commitment and willingness to take a chance

To Mark, young professionals everywhere should study your decision to learn new skills that matter in today's business environment

To Amy, my world changed forever the first time we met and I wouldn't trade it for all the money in the world

To John Ellis and Lucy, chase your dreams but always do it the right way

Contents

What is F.M.L.?

"FML" is often used in pop culture as an off color acronym. In case you missed it, F.M.L. spiked in popularity in 2009 and stood for "F*ck My Life." The term was used by adolescents and 20-somethings to complain about minor daily inconveniences. Spill coffee on your shirt? Why not post a selfie online with the caption "FML."? Parents won't let you go out with your friends? Write a long post on social media and end it with #FML.. Didn't get into your top choice university? It's the end of the world #FML.

Using "FML" as a proclamation of self-pity, gives away control of your life and lets others know you're a passive bystander. Not only am I not a proponent of F.M.L. in this context, but I despise it. The life we have been given should be celebrated and the experiences we have in our lives both good and bad, should be learning experiences not used as mockery.

F.M.L. in the context of this book, is a framework for you to take control of your life. When put into practice, F.M.L. will help you stand out and move forward in your professional life.

The F.M.L. framework consists of 3 stages:

1.   **F - Follow First**. Before you can effectively lead, you must learn to follow.

2.   **M - My Development.** Being a lifelong learner is essential to personal and professional growth. Focusing on you own personal development goes a long way in becoming the best version of yourself you can be.

3.   **L - Lead By Example**. You communicate your ability to lead through your actions. The best way to lead no matter where you are in your career is, by example.

F.M.L. Framework

Lead by Example

The F.M.L. Framework is simple to understand, yet difficult to put into practice. Like many things in life, those who take the challenge and put the framework into action, will get the best results. So the question I pose is, what path will you choose?

Who is This Book For?

There are professionals who work for the weekend. Then there are professionals who love what they do and can't wait for Mondays.

This book can be enjoyed by the people who love Monday's, but this is really for the people who can't wait for the weekend. It's my hope this book provides these people a nudge because I believe in my core, every person can and should add real value to their organization and the world.

It's my belief that the mechanism in which anyone can do this is leadership. Conventional wisdom tells professionals, in order to make the greatest impact on an organization, make more money, and have the best experiences it requires a person to move up the corporate ladder. Truth is a lot of time that is true. What conventional wisdom doesn't tell us is if you aren't prepared for the title once you get it, many times getting promoted can be your worst nightmare.

So this book is about helping professionals who have untapped potential unlock it, and once it's unlocked have them prepared to succeed.

Introduction

The pages in this book are filled with lessons and best practices learned from my professional experience and from hosting the *Follow My Lead* Podcast. It's my hope that at the end of this book you will have learned things to put into practice in your own professional journey. As you read this book keep my two favorite Latin words present in your memory, "Nunc Coepi" (today I begin).

I always believed writing a book was within reach for everyone. In fact, I believe every single person walking the earth should be mandated to write a book as part of our duty as humans. I know it sounds extreme but everyone has a story. Our personal and our professional lives are full of stories. Events and experiences provide the paint for our paintbrush. My book has been trying to come out of me for a while. It has itched and clawed inside my brain for too long. Finally, I was pushed over the edge and forged this book on paper.

The combination of staying up late watching a basketball game between LeBron James and Stephen Curry and a couple of drinks had me in a deep sleep at 4AM. In fact, I was dreaming about the content of this book. These dreams had topics, pictures, and stories so vivid it felt as though F.M.L. was writing itself. I was a bystander in the process and these things were just flowing out of me like a river. The dream was so good, I didn't want it to end. As I was floating through the clouds watching the content of my book come to life, I heard a strange sound. It was a sound I had heard before, but I couldn't quite make it out. I listened harder. It became evident that it was water running. This faint sound of steady stream of liquid wasn't getting louder but it wasn't slowing down. It just kept going and going and going. So much so, that I popped up from my deep sleep opened my eyes.

My 5-year-old, 23 pound, handsome as a devil, King Charles Cavalier had his back leg lifted and was taking a leak on the combination of a desk chair and my hanging shirts. Of course, my lazy dog was too tired at 4AM to get up and go outside to relieve himself. Instead, he did the simplest thing he could do to make that pain go away and jump back up on the bed to find himself a warm spot between my wife and me. As I laid my head back down on the pillow in absolute disbelief and anger that my dog would be so lazy to ruin one of the greatest dreams I've ever had, the nagging feeling to get up and write began.

As a business owner and writer, I had to put those nagging feelings aside many times to catch a little shuteye. As hard as it is, when ideas pop in my mind I had perfected the art of making a note, putting it on my mental to do list for the next day, and working on it when I woke back up at a normal hour. But this was different. This was Relentless. So Relentless, I just had to get up and get the words out of me. So this book is inspired by many people, events, and experiences, but without a lazy King Charles Cavalier it might never have been written.

PART 1

A PROFESSIONAL LIFE OF FULFILLMENT

1

TIME ISN'T LIMITLESS

"When you have balance in your life, work becomes an entirely different experience. There is a passion that moves you to a whole new level of fulfillment and gratitude, and that's when you can do your best... for yourself and for others." - CARA DELEVINGNE

On July 5th 2004, I showed up at the golf course a little more excited than for a regular round of golf. It was an opportunity to spend 4 hours getting back together with a group of friends to enjoy the weather, competition, food, and a day's worth of fun. There was one person I was particularly excited about seeing. As I walked up to the putting green, I saw Chris standing there with a huge smile on his face, as excited about the day as I was. We shook hands gave each other a brotherly hug and picked up right were we had left off. He immediately filled me in on his grades from the previous semester, the friends he made in his fraternity, and the new girl he couldn't get off his mind. The weather was perfect, some trash talking, a few well-played golf shots, and so much laughter we lost track of time. At the end of our round we exchanged a few bucks, slapped hands and went in different directions. Little did I know it was the last time I would see my friend, Chris Rice.

My cell phone rang the morning of July 17th. Chris had been killed in a car accident at 3:30 in the morning at the age of 19. As I fell to my knees in disbelief, all I remember saying was, "He had so much left to do." The next few days were the toughest I have ever experienced. Chris's family was devastated, the driver of the car was devastated, the family of the driver was devastated, Chris' college friends were devastated, his new girlfriend was devastated, and I was devastated.

As the days, weeks, months, and years went by, it didn't get easier. Some days, I questioned God, while others I celebrated the memories Chris and I had together.

13 years later, at every defining life moment, I think of Chris and what he didn't get to experience during his time on this earth. The day I graduated from College and received my diploma, I thought of Chris. The day I watched my wife walk down the aisle, I thought of Chris. The day I took my first job, I thought of Chris. The day my first child was born, I thought of Chris.

But it wasn't until I omit "I" recently that I completely grasped what Chris missed out on so much. I knew he would have thrived and enjoyed the major moments I had experienced, but if Chris had the opportunity to do work he truly loved, he might not have ever stopped. When he found something he liked, he couldn't get enough of it. It was why we both had fallen in love with the game of golf. If Chris could just have had the opportunity to surround himself with bright, funny, talented, and driven people moving in the same direction, towards a worthwhile goal he would have thrived. If Chris could've had the opportunity to spread his love of life to people at work and add value to their lives, I know with 100% certainty he would have loved every minute of it. He would have found wisdom and positivity even in the tough and disappointing times.

Chris never had those opportunities.

_____

Bill Brown loved Motorcycles. It didn't matter the brand or type of motorcycle either; Harley Davidson, Ducati, Mitsubishi, road bike, crotch rocket, or dirt bike. He also loved everything about the powerful machines. The look of them from a distance, the beauty of them up close, the sound as he turned on the ignition, the way it felt when he sat on them, the way the wind blew in his face on the open road, the freedom of leaving the world behind him for that peaceful ride in which no one could get in contact with him. It was his "happy place."

It was just another normal Saturday afternoon when Bill told his wife he was going out for a short ride to be in his "happy place." Neither of them thought much of it, so much so they didn't even kiss goodbye. The ride started out like all the others, but ended much differently. After 20 minutes or so into his ride around the hills of Pennsylvania, he turned on a road he had ridden many times. As he made the turn he saw a view that made all motorcyclist giddy; nothing but sunshine, blue skies and an empty two-lane highway. He gave the bike a little extra gas as the road started downhill. The next thing he knew, he was lying on his back looking up into the big blue sky with completely different thoughts. "Am I alive? Is this heaven? Why can't I move anything?" The 10-15 minutes went by like a blur but the next thing he saw was a police officer leaning down over him. Bill somehow managed to get words out of his mouth that made sense.

Bill: Did I do anything wrong
Officer: No, You were hit by a car that pulled out in front of you at a dangerous intersection at the bottom of the hill. We have had this intersection circled for years to get a blinking light put in but nothing ever happened.
Bill: Can you please tell the driver I forgive her?
Officer: Wow, yes I will.

Bill: Can you please call my wife and tell her I have been in an accident?

Officer: I will have it done right now.

Bill: Can I go hunting this weekend?

Officer: Maybe next season.

Bill: Can you tell if I have any major injuries? I can't feel anything.

Officer: You have some serious injuries that appear to need major medical attention, from what I see right now, you could need an amputation.

Bill: Today is a great day, because I am alive and breathing and God's not done with me, yet.

As Bill said that, the medical staff arrived and swiftly took him away in the ambulance. Multiple surgeries and 11 weeks of hardcore rehab in the hospital followed. During those 11 weeks Bill made a conscious decision to have a positive attitude and use this life changing experience as a positive versus the alternative. To help, he came up with a saying that he would repeat often throughout the day, "upwards and onwards." It didn't take long for nurses and other patients in rehab to be drawn to his positivity. They began saying, "upwards and onwards."

What most people don't know is for many years prior to his accident, Bill Brown had everything going for him from the outside. He was married, a dad to four children, and a Chief Financial Officer for a great company. But inside he had been struggling. Struggling to find fulfillment in his life. Many of the decisions he made were financial, bottom line, and mostly concerned about his own success and well-being. It wasn't until the day that he lay on the pavement, staring up at the sky after a horrific motorcycle accident, that his true perspective changed. Just when he should be only thinking about staying alive his attention turned away from himself and onto others.

Everything in Bill's life changed since he nearly lost his life. It took a catastrophic event for Bill to find purpose and fulfillment. He started to pour his life out into helping others by mentoring, volunteering, spending quality time with his wife and children, writing, and creating a company that supports his new mission. Bill wasn't necessarily unhappy in his 25 years as a CFO, but he wasn't going to let another day go by without living out his new perspective at work. Bill chose to be a leader at the young age of 56 by using his God given gifts into helping others.

Chris Rice and Bill Brown have different stories with different endings. There is much to learn from both of their lives and experiences. However, the most important is that none of us is guaranteed tomorrow.

In my early 20's, I took that saying as a green light to enjoy life, party it up, be selfish, and take from the world. Now, I know the opposite of all of the surface-level stuff is what makes each day we have here valuable. Thinking of others, serving others, sacrificing for a greater cause, mentoring people younger than you, building others up, laughing, smiling with others, helping others through difficult or trying times, this is what making everyday every day count is all about.

Meaningful Work

This book is about what Chris never got to do and what Bill wishes he would have discovered earlier in his life. The work we do can and should have a positive impact on the world. Instead of making us hate or despise life, our work should elevate our lives and the lives of others. Whether you want to admit it or not, all people desire a career of significance and fulfillment. One that makes them excited to get out of bed in the morning because the average person spends over 92,000 hours working in his or her lifetime -- that's the equivalent of 35% of their waking hours. If you are like most professionals, a 40 hour work week is a thing of the past. We are attached to our cell phones, checking email, notifications, and social media 100 times a day. If you can relate, you will work somewhere around 40-45% of your waking hours working. So without being fulfilled in the work you do, it's extremely difficult to be fulfilled in life. It doesn't matter if you are an accountant, banker, sales rep, marketer, product manager, account manager, or the CEO, if you don't begin working towards the meaningful things you will end up working the majority of your life for towards the wrong things, such as money, power or fame. Every single professional deserves to have a career they enjoy.

Most people assume if they can just get a promotion or move their way up the organizational ladder they will be happy and have a career they love. Often times organizational leadership does provide more money and great growth opportunities but if you move into a leadership roles before you have the proper foundation, you actually set yourself up for a less fulfilling career than the alternative. So before you go charging for a promotion let's discover what good leadership really is.

2

CORRECT PERSPECTIVES

"Life has no meaning. Each of us has meaning and we bring it to life. It is a waste to be asking the question when you are the answer" - JOSEPH CAMPBELL

I had been in my sales job for five years and was getting restless. The role had provided such a great training ground but something about it was missing. Yes, the products I sold were helping improve people's careers, but I wasn't fulfilled. I longed for deeper meaning in my work.

It took some searching. The answers didn't come easily, but I finally figured out what was missing. When I was helping other people improve – whether I was offering a friend guidance in their life or helping a coworker through a difficult sales slump, I felt a spark. When I thought about how I could achieve this feeling at work, becoming an organization leader seemed like the best answer.

If I could find a way to get promoted and manage a team of people, it would allow me to experience this spark on a daily basis. It would allow me to move from producing for myself to helping others produce.

Instead of mentally checking out of my current sales role or applying for jobs at another organizations, I decided to make it happen in my current organization by being so good they couldn't ignore me. Just like anything good in life, you can't skip to the end and expect great results, so I knew had to put in the work. My goal changed from making my targets each month, to being the top sales performer. Luckily things fell into place and I got the opportunity I was seeking.

I thought becoming a leader of a team in the professional world would come naturally considering all the leadership roles I'd held before – captain of the football team, class president, captain of the golf team, etc. I couldn't have been more wrong. Everything about leading people in an organization was challenging. What made leadership so challenging was that I really didn't know what it was and while I thought I knew what it was all about I didn't have a clue.

However, your journey or desire to move into organizations leadership is probably different than mine. Either way, here we are meeting on this journey. I do know everyone views leadership differently, so let's create some level ground.

One of the best ways to grasp leadership is first by looking at the common myths around it. When I say myths think of just some common myths that you might have been taught or believe to be true.

- Drinking soda and PopRocks at the same time will kill you
- St. Patrick was Irish
- Cutting and an earthworm in half, will create two earthworms

...All of those are myths.

It can be hard to differentiate fact from fiction when these myths are passed down by well-intentioned people or the almighty internet.

So, I'd like **you** to consider the validity of what you've learned about leadership up until today.

You may have heard myths about leadership like...

"Leaders are born, not made"
The argument about whether Leaders are born or made has been debated for many years. It's as timeless as the debate "what came first, the chicken or the egg."

But what does science say? A recent study by the "The Leadership Quarterly" showed that leadership is 24 percent genetic and 76 percent learned. So, yes... people are born with some innate qualities that predispose them to being leaders; however, those qualities will only get you so far. Which means, anybody can develop into a leader who that creates business results and improves the lives of those around them. Which leads me to the second myth...

"Being a leader is only for certain types of people"

We all put our pants on one leg at a time. Leadership positions are within reach for anyone regardless of what school you attended, where you grew up, who your parents are, your ethnicity, past mistakes, and anything else that's kept you from believing in yourself.

"A title makes a leader"

"People follow people, not titles." It's that simple. How many "managers" or "executives" have you encountered who are horrible leaders of people? Conversely, how many amazing people have you met who don't hold titles? It's the person, not the title that defines a leader.

Here's one last myth for you: **"Leaders control, micromanage, and are authoritative**."
This is perhaps the worst myth of all. There are many

different leadership styles, but all the great leaders have one thing in common – they empower others. They find ways to bring people with them, rather than manipulating or pushing in the direction they want them to go.

While it's important you acknowledge all of these are myths, the key point is: what exactly is leadership, if it's not those things?

There have been hundreds if not thousands of definitions of leadership, one of my personal favorites is one that I came about through an interview I had with Peter Browning, the former CEO of National Gypsum. He had a definition of leadership that blew me away. It's made such an impact on me I memorized it that night.

"The capacity to elicit the willing collaboration of others towards a worthwhile goal over and an extended period of time." As I have reflected over this definition it's clear to me that his definition is perfect for a CEO. So I want you to keep this written down somewhere to reflect on at times as you progress in your career.

The most famous definition of leadership comes from John Maxwell who says "Leadership is Influence." While John's definition is true, I have found it to be too simple.

The definition that sums up leadership in the easiest most implementable way, regardless your role, comes from a former President of the United States, John Quincy Adams:

"If your actions inspire others to dream more, learn more, do more, and become more, you are a leader."

Adams' definition was simply way ahead of his time because his words were seconded in the modern day by Microsoft founder Bill Gates:

"As we look ahead into the next century, leaders will be those who empower others."

To sum it up, leadership is about serving others and helping others become the best version they can be. In other words, 'if serving is below you, leadership is beyond you.' There are countless examples of men and women throughout history who have lived out leadership in their professional and personal lives. Some of which you will read about throughout the book. The key is, no matter what you do professionally in your life, if you can keep this mindset of helping and serving others, you drastically improve your chances of making an impact on the world and being fulfilled in your professional life.

The best part is, serving and thinking about others is a

choice we make like many others in our lives. We make massive choices like where we go to college, who we marry, where we live, what profession we pursue, or what kind of parent we are. We make small choices like what we eat, what car we drive, how we respond to an event, or what show we pick out on Netflix.

So this begs the question if we choose to serve like all of these others choices, do we choose leadership? If so, which category does it fall into: big or small; trivial or significant?

Leadership is a choice you make just like any other and it's a big choice. What's interesting is it just takes accepting and realizing you are a leader and that you have leadership within you. With that leadership from within you are meant to influence others. As you grow and become the best version of yourself, you are then able to help others become the best version of themselves. As you continually do this you will make a difference and be a better leader.

A recent survey showed that 40% of modern professionals want to serve in a leadership capacity. Not only is this percentage small, but according to Deloitte, 86% of organizations don't believe their leadership pipeline is "very ready." This puts professionals and organizations in a difficult position because it shows:

1. Not enough people want to choose leadership
2. Even if you do choose leadership, you may not be deemed "ready" by your employers.

The solution is simple. We need more people just like you choosing leadership. Choosing to serve, choosing to inspire others to dream more, learn more, do more and become more. Choosing to impact others' lives in a positive way and not being scared to make the big and tough decisions that leads to opportunities for many not just a few. Leadership is for everyone. The world needs more leaders, your company needs more leaders, your family needs more leaders, and your friends need more leaders... not less.

3

IT'S ABOUT THE PEG

"In every day, there is **1,440** minutes. That means we have **1,440** daily opportunities to make a positive impact." - **LES BROWN**

If I told you I knew a surefire way for you to expand your knowledge, have the opportunity to travel, and earn more money would that pique your interest? What would you pay to find out what it was? How far would you go to find it? How many web searches would you do until you came up empty trying to find a PDF on the internet about my secret?

Instead of going to all the trouble, I am going to share it with you here. But before I do, let me tell you how I discovered it.

On a September afternoon in 2013, I was sitting in my office looking out the window daydreaming about doing any job outside. It was one of those 75 degree days, not a cloud in the sky, just tormenting me for being inside. The thoughts ran through my mind over and over, "this just isn't fair." My daydream session quickly came to an end when there was a knock on the door. As I quickly turned around I saw the manager of another business unit. We didn't interact often, as he traveled a great deal, but I always was interested in what he had to say. He lived a life of adventure, financial success, and was always talking about the latest thing he learned. After a few pleasantries, he made me aware that he was leaving to pursue opportunities outside of the company. As he shook my hand and walked out of the room, I it came to me. If he was leaving, I wanted his job.

I strategized and planned how I could stand out enough with the upper level management to not only be considered for the opening but to make it so compelling they couldn't say no. Day after day, I put in extra work. I made 5 more prospecting calls a day, sent double the amount of emails, did more research into my current opportunities, and began a sales blog. The focus on the process turned into results. In one day, I closed two opportunities totaling over $600,000 in revenue for the company. While I was excited about the deals closing, I was more excited because I finally had proof to show why I was the guy for the job. In the beginning of December of that year, I pitched the idea to the CEO and CFO. I was set on moving out of my current sales role to take over the business unit. They were not only receptive to the idea, they were waiting for someone to step up to the plate and fill the void.

What followed was an opportunity that paid more money, provided new experiences, and grew me as a professional. Thus the not-so-secret secret came about, Organizational Leadership.

PEG Factor

Overtime I developed the PEG Factor to convey the value of moving up and becoming a leader in your organization. In the PEG Factor, P+E+G = Fulfillment

Providing
+
Experience
+
Growth
=
Fulfillment

P = Providing

Statistics show that providing financially for yourself and/or your family is the most important component in order for a professional to be fulfilled by their job. Each individual's financial threshold is different, but a Princeton study found that once an individual is making $75,000, the majority of their happiness that is derived from money (the ability to provide) is fulfilled. But it's not totally about the dollar amount, Providing is tied to your expectations and standard of living required to feel fulfilled. If you are only driven by money, it will never be enough. Consider how much money you want to make to support your lifestyle and stick within it.

E = Experiences

A large part of fulfillment at work is having positive experiences. Whether it's completing a difficult project, feeling appreciated by your colleagues, traveling to industry conferences, giving a presentation to a group, or hiring an employee, positive experiences add to our fulfillment at work.

G = Growth

William Butler Yeats said it best, "we are happy, when we are growing." When you are acquiring new skills, given challenging work, and adding value -- you are growing. You should answer in 5 seconds whether you are growing in your current job.

Providing + Experiences + Growth = Fulfillment.

If you are providing, having positive experiences, and growing professionally, you will be fulfilled in your work. These are all measured by YOUR EXPECTATIONS. If any of those factors aren't equal to your expectation, there's a high likelihood that you will become one of the $2/3^{rds}$ of professionals who are anticipated to switch jobs in the next 5 years.

So what does the PEG Factor have to do with becoming a leader? The role of being a leader within an organization typically provides the opportunity to increase each element of the PEG Factor. And hopefully, if you fully grasp the importance of the PEG Factor, you will ensure you're helping your people become fulfilled as well.

The PEG Factor At Work

A popular high-growth startup company was developing so fast, it was hiring people 20- 30 at a time. The CEO quickly realized the need to have an additional layer of management, but he knew the pitfalls of just promoting top performers. He came up with a clever way to incent the right people for these new positions. He held company-wide meeting asking for those interested in these new leadership positions to email him by the end of the week. But he also made it clear that the leadership position included a few additional work trips a year, but didn't include a pay increase. What happened next was amazing. Only 4 people out of a company of hundreds raised their hand wanting to move into this new role. Four people who wanted to lead for the sake of leading and helping others, not for their own financial gain. The experiment worked by discovering those who wanted the role for new experiences and personal growth. In the end, the CEO had something up his sleeve --the new leaders also received a pay increase.

This is a perfect example of how 4 individuals who moved into new leadership positions and improved their personal PEG. They increased their pay (providing), had new work experiences (travel), and managed others (growth).

I often get a chance to meet with young professionals and I use the PEG factor to help them determine their expectations in the areas of Providing, Experiences and Growth.

If you go through the activity on your own, here's a guide:

Providing

What are your expectations for providing? How much money do you need to make to support your lifestyle and how much money do you want to make to fulfill personal ambitions? Write both numbers down, add 10% to both numbers and you have defined how much money you need to be making in order to be fulfilled financially in your work.

For Example:

NEED: $75,000 + 10% = $82,500

WANT: $250,000 + 10% = $275,000

Why add 10%? Giving away 10% of your money is a great way to serve others.

In the example above, the person should focus on making between $82,500 and $275,000 a year and giving away 10% to be fulfilled in their work to be aligned to their earnings expectations.

Experiences

What are your expectations of experiences? Many of our best memories in our personal lives come from the experiences we have in life such as weddings, attending a concert or a live sporting event. The same is true at work. We need experiences at work to be fulfilled. What are some experiences you want? Examples included: hiring someone, running an internal or client meeting, or attending an industry conference. Everyone desires different experiences; you have to determine what you want. Write them down or simply think about experiences you desire that you either want to repeat or have not yet had.

Growth

What are your expectations of Growth? Anytime people are developing new skills, learning new jobs or getting more responsibility they are growing. How do you want to grow? Is it learning to write code, starting a podcast for your company, a personal or company YouTube channel, or simply moving into a different role? Write down how you want to grow, things that would challenge you professionally and take you out of your comfort zone.

4

THE JOURNEY WORTH TAKING

"The journey of a thousand miles begins with one step" - CHINESE PROVERB

Abraham Lincoln is widely considered to be one of the greatest presidents of the United States. Consider his accomplishments, including keeping the Union together during the Civil War and signing the Emancipation Proclamation to put an end to slavery. By all accounts he was an exceptional leader, husband, father, Christian and mentor during his life. But what's often left out of the story of President Lincoln is the path of obstacles and the pain he encountered in his life prior to being elected president.

At the age of 9 his mother died. At the age of 23, he lost his job and was defeated for the first time in a bid for state legislature. One year later, he and a partner started a business that failed miserably and left him in debt for over 17 years. Two years after, his fiancé died unexpectedly. The next year, he had a nervous breakdown, leaving him immovable from his house for nearly two years. He picked himself back up at the age of 28, but was defeated for speaker of Illinois. Five years later he lost his nomination for Congress. His next losses came when he was rejected for an appointment to the US Land Office as well as being beaten during his run for a US Senate Seat.

Things started to look up a few years later when Lincoln became a candidate for the Vice Presidency, but the excitement was short-lived when he was again defeated. Not to be stopped, he again ran for the US Senate 2 years later, and if you're picking up on the trend you can guess what happened next (he lost)! Things weren't much better in Lincoln's personal life. During this time, he suffered the loss of two young sons, ages 3 and 12.

If you weren't keeping track, prior to ever being elected President of the Unites of America at the age of 51, Lincoln was defeated or rejected for public office 7 times! We will never know what was going on the heart and mind of Lincoln during those years of defeat, but he had a solid foundation of patience, proactivity and courage.

So no matter what you do professionally, if you want to stand out from the crowd, move up, and make an impact in your organization and the world, all three of these elements must be present.

Patience

Growing up, the saying "patience is a virtue" wasn't just an adage, it was a fact. Of all the lessons I teach my kids, this one is at the top of the list. I can't image Abraham Lincoln's feelings and emotions during all of his years of heartbreak. But his ability to stay patient and know there was a bigger plan for his life is a true testament to his character. Many of us struggle with patience, but with good reason. Being patient feels awful and challenging. On a daily basis, we want things when we want them. And more and more, we're able to scratch our instant gratification itch – which also means we are practicing patience even less. When we have to be patient for the big things like professional progress, we literally have to use a muscle that's atrophied from years of laziness. Maybe you've had a plan for your life? Go to college, graduate, get a job, move up the corporate ladder, get married, have 3 kids and be in upper-level management by the time you're 35 years old. Sounds nice. Having goals and plans are an excellent way to structure your life, but you also have to navigate through the unforeseen. This requires, you guessed it, patience. When you have challenging moments where your path doesn't appear to be a straight line, remind yourself (as cheesy as it sounds), "patience is a virtue." And remind yourself of Lincoln's challenges and accomplishments.

Proactivity

There was once a grasshopper who loved life. He spent his time lazing in the sun, eating when he wanted to, sleeping when he wanted to, generally enjoying himself all the time. He lived like he did not have a care in the world.

One day as he was sun-bathing, he saw an ant pushing a bread crumb across the ground. The grasshopper asked, "Hey brother! What are you doing?" The ant replied, "I am gathering food for the winter while the weather is still warm. Once winter sets in, I am going to stay home and just eat from my stock of food."

The grasshopper made fun of the ant's dull life and went on sun bathing saying, "There's enough time for such boring work. You should take time to have fun like me." Soon the summer passed and the winter started to set in.

As the weather became colder, it became harder for the grasshopper to get out. However, he soon started to feel hungry. He decided to brave the weather and find himself some food.

When he stepped out, everything was covered with snow and he could not find anything to eat. He continued to search for food everyday. He did not find anything. Finally, he grew weak and died of hunger.

Just like the grasshopper, you can have all the patience in the world but without being proactive and going for it, your gift of patience might never become a positive. In fact it actually might hurt your career.

What I didn't tell you about President Lincoln is that during those 7 rejections from public office that spanned over a 28 year period, he didn't sit and wait around for the next election cycle; he was proactive. He was a postmaster, earned a law degree, practiced law, won smaller elections, got married, had children, gave back to his community, and worked hard on his faith walk.

Courage
Desmond Doss' faith and religious beliefs didn't allow him to carry a gun or threaten another human life. This became an issue when Doss was drafted into the United States military to fight in WWII. He was a conscientious objector, placed as a non-combatant. Doss was the constant target of jokes from other soldiers. He was stationed as field medic in Okinawa. One day, the Japanese attacked his unit on the top of a cliff. Nearly every man was hurt or wounded. Doss proceeded to rig up a stretcher. By himself and under fire, he retrieved every soldier and returned them to safety. Doss was presented with the Medal of Honor from the President

Truman. His story eventually was made into the Oscar Nominated film, Hacksaw Ridge.

Courage is the ability to do something that frightens you. In order for you to do anything meaningful in your career, you will have to step out on a limb and do things that scare you or better yet have a high likelihood of failure.

You don't have to emulate Doss to be seen as courageous. Courage could be you standing up for a coworker when they have been wronged, taking on a new challenge in your company when you don't know if you're ready (or the odds look against you). Leading others requires courage.

Your Time Will Come

It was a soul crushing feeling. I had worked so hard, believed I was doing everything right, and it was now evident that the promotion wasn't going to happen. My dream of leading a team wasn't going to become a reality today. As I sat with my head in my hands I couldn't figure out if I wanted to cry, pray, or go to the bar.

Then, I felt a hand of a mentor on my shoulder. He leaned down and whispered: *"Your Time Will Come."*

* * *

Not only was that the last thing I wanted to hear, but it made me more upset. Instead of voicing my opinion, I just left my head in my hands and let him leave the room. Over the next few days, I managed to avoid the tears and drowning my sorrow at a bar. Instead, I allowed his words to really sink in. I started to believe he was right, but he wasn't just right about me, he was right about everyone.

One of the questions I get asked most often from modern professionals is, "Am I on the right path?" and "If I am on the right path, when will my time come?" Here are some signs that will let you know your time is coming:

You Have Found the Right Passion

For years, I did a job that I liked, but didn't love. The afternoons were long and left me constantly daydreaming about the upcoming weekend. It wasn't until I discovered my passion for leadership development, writing, and helping others on their leadership journey that I realized what I was missing.

Passion is the willingness to suffer for something you love. There are so many professionals who aren't willing to suffer for their work. What's worse is many people suffer for a job they can't stand. Most people think the key word is "passion" but the key word is actually "right."

People can find passion in sports, games, etc. but those aren't typically things that can make a big impact on others. You will know your passion is "right" when you begin to make a positive impact on others.

Your Patience for More Experience

We live in an instant gratification world that pretty much provides us everything we want, "Right now." Unfortunately that's not what happens on the path to leadership. In order to be successful in whatever you do, don't be afraid of experience first. The world makes us believe we are ready for more responsibility than we actually are. There are many reasons people are in their current roles. Maybe your current role is setting you up for being really successful in your next role. The key is that you are willing to gain the experience and maintain enough patience to delay immediate gratification.

Your Willingness to Do What Others are Not

The CEO of SAP, Bill McDermott, started his professional journey by scraping together every penny he had to open a small deli on Long Island. Bill knew his only chance to create a successful business was to be willing to do what other big stores were not. So he stocked the store with products not offered from his big store competitors, added video game room that wouldn't typically be in a deli, and delivered food to the elderly.

All of these things weren't things Bill's store had to do to be successful. They were things that he knew the larger stores wouldn't be able or willing to do. Bill's small entrepreneurial success story is completely relevant to determining if "your time is coming."

The professionals who have a willingness to do what others are not, separate themselves for the crowd. This society we currently live in tells us the opposite. "If you don't want to do it or don't feel like doing it, don't do it" or "if it doesn't feel good then why do it?" Unfortunately this sends a terrible message and example of what actually separates those from others.

Continued Development of Personal Grit

Angela Duckworth wrote a book called *Grit* that opened my eyes. I don't know if it's scientifically proven, but I believe the #1 predictor and factor of success is grit. Grit is the ability to work hard over a long period of time towards a worthwhile goal. It allows us to keep moving forward in the face of obstacles, adversity, or misfortune.

In order for you to keep moving forward when someone says, "Your time will come," you must have grit. So no matter where you are in your professional journey, it's paramount you are doing challenging things that have a high likelihood of failure. The best way to continue to develop grit is to try, fail, and then try again.

Maturity to Understand, "It Isn't All About You"

Looking back 8 years, it's crystal clear why I didn't succeed in reaching my dream of being a successful pro golfer on the PGA Tour. My world revolved around me, and I was concerned about #1 virtually 24 hours a day. If I had success at that time in my life, I wouldn't have been prepared to handle it. Once you begin to attribute the positives in your life to people other than yourself, you're on your way to becoming someone worthy of followers.

Intense Focus on the Process Not the Results

Nick Saban, head football coach for the Alabama Crimson Tide, is famous for his commitment to the PROCESS. He is relentless in keeping his team and coaching staff focused on the things that they are able to control. These things include, but are not limited to, effort, execution, and teamwork. It's nearly impossible to produce good results when that's all you're focused on. The more you can immerse yourself into the process of what produces results the better off you will be.

What's interesting is, even if you do all of these really well you still aren't guaranteed an arrival time, but I do believe your time will come. Keeping the mindset that you are destined for great things and having faith that good things are coming is paramount. So , instead of looking at your clock, waiting for your "time to come," spend it focused on the things you can control - like the F.M.L. Framework.

PART 2

THE FRAMEWORK FOR MOVING UP AND BEING A LEADER

5

THE F.M.L. FRAMEWORK

"You don't have to be a genius or a visionary or even a college graduate to be successful. You just need a framework and a dream" - MICHAEL DELL

I knew immediately something was wrong. Her shoulders slumped a little, she was walking slower than normal and as I looked into her eyes you could start to see tears beginning to form. I quickly pulled her aside and asked, "Can you tell me what's going on?" Before she could even get out a word, the tears began to stream and her head dropped. As I gave her a hug, I sensed relief as she let it all go. After a couple minutes she composed herself and opened up about the situation. "I just don't know what to do, I feel unappreciated, I don't feel challenged here at work, the team members who are more senior than me treat me poorly. I know in my heart I am capable of doing so much to help this team be successful, but nothing I have done up until this point mattered. I just don't know if what I am doing is right, but I love this company and I want to help more."

Before I responded I chose my words carefully since she

wasn't on my team. "You are such a talented professional who has so much to give not only to this company but to the community. Just a year into my professional journey I was sitting at a conference table surrounded by 5 people for a meeting and not more than 30 minutes into that meeting I was in uncontrollable tears. It was one of the most embarrassing days of my career to date. So let's start by saying you are already way ahead of me by pulling it together and crying just between us and not in front of 5 high level executives. Next, you're still alive, you weren't fired, and you will learn a lot from this. Look at this moment as a positive. Your professional career is a journey, think of the long game -- what doesn't kill you, will only make you stronger."

She looked up at me she cracked a smile. I continued, "Everything experienced and will experience at this company can and will make you a better professional throughout your career if you want it to. If you can keep a positive mindset, you will always be growing and helping your career's long game. Your career is a long-term investment, not day trading. Most people who believe in overnight successes are foolish. If you show me someone who has achieved great things today, I could easily show you they were working for 5-10 years before they ever were recognized."

Her response was perfect, "Thank you, that's exactly what I needed to hear."

I finished by saying, "There is an important concept and framework that helped me progress faster in my career and be better prepared to be a leader worth following. Would you like to know what it is?"

"Absolutely! Is it that F.M.L. thing you've mentioned before? I hope it doesn't mean what I think."
"It sure is... and no, it doesn't mean what you think."

F.M.L. Framework

What I described to her that evening is what I am going to share with you now. F.M.L. is a framework you can use that includes a collection of best practices and ideas that follow a natural progression. Unfortunately, professional progress and leadership aren't destinations you can pinpoint on a map. There aren't step-by-step or turn-by-turn directions to ensure you are in a leadership position at a certain date. But having these fundamental concepts in place will help you stand out and move up. If you use this framework and the elements within it, you will create your own unique path to leadership and be better prepared to effectively lead others.

The best part is, the framework is simple to remember. It's "F-M-L"! No, it's probably not the first thing that came to your mind... but I bet you'll remember it now. F.M.L. stands for "Follow My Lead" and here's what the framework stands for:

F – Follow First
M – My Development
L – Lead by Example

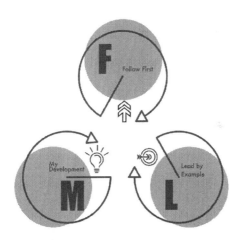

Follow. Follow First

Most people think of a follower as someone who is weak or unable to lead. Quite the opposite is true. In order for you to be a great leader, it starts with first being an active follower. The key word there is active. Active followers understand this stage of their professional journey is about learning, gaining experience, and ultimately turning these two things into expertise. I don't know one person who has become a great leader without first being an active follower.

My. My Development

A focus on your personal growth will help you become the best possible professional and person you can be. Once you take ownership of your own development, you will have the opportunity to truly turn the corner and perform at levels you can't even imagine. Being tuned-into your development is critical to aligning yourself with people and activities that will enhance your professional progress and potential impact.

Lead. Lead By Example

The choices you make every single day will be watched and judged by others whether you like it or not. This means you have the ability to earn credibility and build trust through your actions. At the end of the day, you have to earn the right to lead and you can do this through leading by example. People will create a perception of you based on how you lead by example and it will have an enormous impact on your ability to create traction and momentum in your professional progress. Most people believe they don't have control over the perception others have of them. While it's true you can't control someone else's brain, you have much more control over people's perception of you than you probably believe.

As a by-product of implementing the F.M.L. framework, you will also improve your personal and professional life. So I am putting the ball in your court and challenging you to take what's in the rest of this book and put it into action.

It's Up to You, But Here is a Head Start

There was a study done not long ago to determine the best way to transfer knowledge to a group of student to ensure knowledge was retained and implemented 6 weeks after an instructor-led workshop. The study was simple; the total number of learners was broken into 3 groups. All the groups received the same 4 hour instructor-led training session, but the reinforcement was different for each groups. The first group received a 4 hour training session and was sent on their way with no additional follow up for 6 weeks. The second group received the same 4 hour session but was provided ongoing reinforcement once a week for 6 weeks via email. The last group was provided the same 4 hour session, but was asked to answer active questions every day for 6 weeks. The results of the study were staggering. The third group outperformed the other groups by over

60% in a test given at the end of the 6th week. The results tied directly to the active questions about implementation of the content.

If you aren't familiar, active questions are those in which a person grades themselves every day to determine how well they did something. As an example "Did I implement what I learned?" "Did I do my best today?

The reason the knowledge stuck was because the students took personal ownership and rated themselves on how well they knew and performed what they learned. So before we get into the F.M.L. framework, there are two questions I want you to get into a habit of asking yourself each day (and hopefully for weeks or months to come):

1. "Did I do my best today?"
2. "Did I implement what I learned from F.M.L. today?"

I know this seems simple but when you take a self-reflective view of how hard you worked in these two areas by simply answering the two questions with an honest "Yes" or "No," you begin to take ownership of your development as a professional. Some of the best ways I have seen people remind themselves of these two questions are by:

- • Writing them on a whiteboard
- • Setting an alarm or reminder on your phone at the same time each day
- • Writing them on a 3 x 5 note card

Make the commitment to use active questions at least until you finish this book. Before you turn the page, all I ask is you figure out what your method of answering these two questions is going to be. Once you have it, then it's time to jump into the first element of the F.M.L. Framework.

6

FOLLOW FIRST

"I am reminded how hollow the label of leadership sometimes is and how heroic followership can be." - WARREN BENNIS

Skip Allison was a rising star in his company. In two short years he had become a top performer and he was well-liked among his peers. Skip had one major issue; he didn't get along well with his immediate boss. There was a constant battle for power and attention.

In one meeting, he was told he had to execute an internal process that made no sense to him. Skip walked out of the group meeting because he couldn't handle his emotions. The CEO of Skip's company wanted to try and uncover what was really going on and brought me in as a coach.

It was evident within minutes of my first meeting with Skip the problem had nothing to do with his will to be successful. Instead, it was about his skill to follow. Skip walked through multiple scenarios in which he openly admitted to his struggle with conforming to authority. He thought he knew enough after two years and didn't need his boss. He believed he would be better off if the company left him on his own to do his job. What I said next to Skip is something he consistently mentions to me years later changed the trajectory of his career, "If you can't learn to follow, you will never be able to lead."

After multiple coaching sessions, I finally got Skip to think about the power of becoming a good follower. In our final session we covered the three most important parts of following. He actually got a kick out of them and could remember them easily because the acronym we used to remember them was LOL. Most people think of LOL as 'laugh out loud,' but in our case it stands for listening, obedience, and learning.

Listening
I know it's a cliché, but ACTUALLY listen when other

people are talking. It sounds simple, but how often are you already thinking about what you will say next before another person has finished talking? Or how often do you interrupt them to interject your thoughts? How often do you have your phone in your hand when someone is talking and you take a quick glance at in an incoming text or vibration? The truth is we are all guilty of these things, but they are signs of a bad listener. People know when you are actually listening to them. If you need proof just think about the last time you were talking to a friend about an important topic. I am sure you knew they were listening and cared about what you were saying within 10 seconds. Listening is something that requires a lot of practice and constant attention because it's an art that's being lost to all the other noise around us.

Obedience

When most people hear the word 'obedience' it has a negative connotation. The actual definition of obedience is compliance with an order, request, or law or submission to another authority. There is absolutely nothing weak or negative about compliance or submission to authority. Most people are compliant about or submit to many things that are meant to be helpful to us. The best example is drinking and driving. The laws are put into place not to arrest and prosecute those who don't obey the law; they are put in place for the safety of every single person on the road. Most of us freely choose to obey these laws because we care about our own safety and the safety of others on the road. If you choose to not be obedient to the laws around drinking and driving there are consequences either by law enforcement or worse life or death. Obedience isn't weak anymore is it?

Every single rule or process at your work isn't going to be as life or death as drinking and driving but obedience in the workplace is important. Sure there will be times to push back or disagree with authority, but until you are obedient to the rules laid out for you, you won't receive the same amount of respect.

Learning

"Never stop learning because life never stops teaching."
– Unknown

Being a follower provides learning opportunities much more regularly than leading. If you have a learning mindset as a follower, you get to learn from everything around you. The things you like and don't like, ways you would lead better or differently, and life lessons to apply the rest of your life.

So the next time you see someone write LOL, let it remind you to be a good follower first.

Experience vs. Expertise

As the client meeting commenced I knew the team had high expectations for the next two hours. The outcome of the meeting was either going to lead to a big win for the company or quite possibly the biggest loss in our history. As we sat down in the big conference room, Kelly sat to my left and Timothy to my right. Kelly had just joined the team a year ago and Timothy had nearly 20 years of experience in the industry. We had a large part of the meeting set aside for Timothy to present the slides because of his experience. As Tim began speaking through the first 10 slides it quickly became evident that the presentation wasn't moving in the direction that I wanted. As I started to slide my chair back to stand up and interrupt, Kelly spoke up. "Timothy I would like to stop on this slide about social learning for a minute and explain exactly why this is so important in today's competitive business marketplace. While most people have a hard time arguing against this concept in theory, its power is in what's actually happening in the world around us. Millennials, like myself, now make up the largest percentage of the workforce. This is relevant because we communicate both inside and outside of work on social networks. Just think about it this for a second. My primary method of communication with my friends is Snapchat. Almost all of my professional friends log into LinkedIn once a day and are active at some level by interacting and helping other professionals do their job better. Why would you not take the same approach?"

As Kelly wrapped up her engaging and relevant story the CEO on the other end of the table cleared her throat and said, "That is exactly what I have been thinking, I just didn't know how to express it. I see all of our young employees doing the same thing as you just described. Tell me more about exactly how you see this working in our organization."

It was the green light everyone on our team was hoping to hear during the meeting - an invitation to share some ideas to help the prospective client. The best part was it didn't happen because of Timothy's 20 years of experience, it happened because of a young professional who used her *expertise* at just the right time. Kelly is what I call an Active Follower. She doesn't sit back waiting for those above her to lay out every detail of her day or what they want her to do. She grasps her current role, and she is relentless in her pursuit of industry and business knowledge. She consistently relates it to our organization on an ongoing basis. She is always trying new ideas and exploring different ways to help us grow.

If Kelly's example wasn't enough to convince you of the

importance of being an Active Follower in order to gain expertise, there are others benefits that will help you throughout your career and when you are leading a team.

Awareness of Others

Organizational leaders constantly deal with both adversaries and allies. One of the very best ways to understand what others want, need and or desire is from being an active follower. Learning to be aware of others will pay dividends, not only in your professional journey, but also in your personal life.

The Art of Tact

Without a doubt, the art of tact is a skill great leaders leverage on a daily basis. One of my favorite stories about the importance of Tact comes from Brian Cavanaugh. He told this story to describe its essence.

A Sultan called in one of his seers and asked how long he would live. "Sire," said the seer, "you would live to see all your sons dead." The sultan flew into a rage and handed the prophet over to his guards for execution.

He then called for a second seer, and asked him the same question. "Sire," said the prophet, "I see you blessed with long life, so long that you will outlive all your family." The sultan was delighted and rewarded this seer with gold and silver jewelry.

Both prophets knew the truth, but one had tact, the other did not.

Brian's story of the Sultan and the sire puts tact into perspective and why it's so important. There are opportunities in the workplace every single day where acting in a tactful way can make all the difference in a positive vs. negative outcome. As an example, it's difficult not seeing eye to eye with coworkers. By being an Active Follower First, you will have the opportunity to learn how to develop your tact to navigate relationships and disagreements. The better you get at this art of tact, the better prepared you will be to manage differences of opinion and personality.

The Ability to Think Critically

By being a good Active Follower tasks are often delegated to you. Think critically about how to execute these tasks in the fastest, most efficient and effective way possible. These tasks are your opportunity to become a problem solver. Something that all great leaders have the ability to do, which means they learned a lot of this from right in this position.

Leadership Compound Theory

It didn't take long to figure out that Jeremy thought highly of himself. He had been at the company six whole weeks and it was abundantly clear that he was focused on #1. It started from the minute he walked in the door and continued throughout the day. He rarely said hello to others in passing, in meetings he always started his sentences with "I" instead of "we," he made no bones about how great he thought he was and how quickly he was going to achieve his next goal.

About the same time Jeremy started at the company, Grace was also hired. Grace was the polar opposite. She was constantly asking others what she could do to help, never over promised and under delivered. But she had other struggles. She would get dumped on, over-scheduled, and made to do tasks no one else wanted to do – every time. People were taking advantage of her kindness.

I knew that if I could bring out Grace's strengths in Jeremy and vice versa they would become almost irreplaceable assets to our team. So I sat them both down in our conference room and started drawing on the whiteboard.

I started with Jeremy and asked him, "What's your biggest strength as a professional?" Without hesitation he said, "confidence. I have a ton of self-belief and I don't want others to slow me down. Instead of responding I simply drew two circles and wrote confidence in one."

Then I asked him to describe his attitude towards career progressions. "Well I have a tremendous amount of drive. I wake up in the morning at 5:30 without an alarm clock ready to get my day started and achieve the goals I set for myself." Without hesitation I wrote "Drive" in the other circle.

"These two elements of 'confidence' and 'drive' together are what we call the 'Cocky Compound." For weeks Jeremy, your teammates have come to me individually to tell me how much they have struggled to work with you and how you make them feel less than important. People with only this compound usually get things done, they typically think about themselves more than the group, they elevate within organizations quickly, but they are rarely viewed as leaders by those they manage – even if they're promoted. They may create results for themselves, but rarely create results for others. At the end of the day: people are only capable of achieving so much all by themselves so this compound is dangerous to stay in for a long period of time in your career."

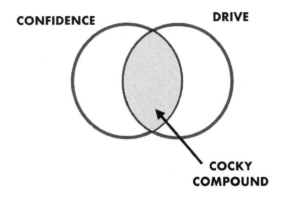

CONFIDENCE **DRIVE**

COCKY COMPOUND

Just about this time Grace piped up and said, "Well, why I am I here? I don't fit the cocky compound at all." I replied, "Grace you are exactly right." And I drew two more circles on the board. "If your teammates had to describe you in one word, what do you think would be their answer?" She paused for a moment and said, "Selfless. I always try to help others first and not think about myself." I turned to the board and wrote, selflessness in the third circle. Instead of turning around and asking any more questions I wrote "character" in the last remaining circle. As I turned around I said, "Character is why everyone on this team was hired in the first place, without character people don't have a place here. Together, Selfless and Character create the "cordial compound." These people have great hearts, they care about others, they stand for certain qualities – so much so that they at times get taken advantage of – or are passed up for management positions because they're not thought of as leaders."

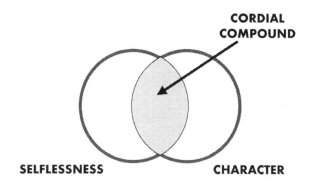

"Grace, as I watch you work, I can see people taking advantage of you without your knowledge. While I don't want you to look at your strengths as negatives, these are powerful qualities that make me believe in your ability to become a leader here at this company."

"Now, there are good and bad elements about both compounds, but neither one of makes up a true leader. Here's the cool part. When these 4 elements come together, they create a new something new – what I call the "Leader Compound."

"Here is the tricky part, it's very difficult to have all four elements present – it's like trying to get two opposing forces to come together – like two magnets that are positively charged. The people that grasp the magnitude of these four elements and intentionally combine them every day, will not only stand out as a potential leader, they'll excel as one."

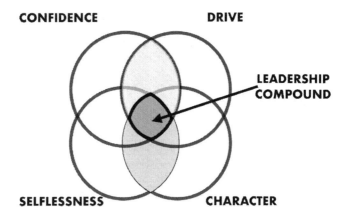

Jeremy then piped up and said, "I didn't know what to expect when I came into this meeting but I really like the Leadership Compound Theory because I know where I need to put in the work. I can target becoming selfless and better develop my character. Can you go through each element individually and explain ways to improve in each area? Even the areas of Confidence and Drive I am sure I could improve as well." As I took a deep breathe, I said, "I thought you would never ask, let's get into each one individually."

Confidence

Confidence gives us the power and belief that we can conquer the world. Confident people typically face their fears head-on and tend to be risk-takers. Barrie Davenport said it best "Low self-confidence isn't a life sentence. Self-confidence can be learned, practiced and mastered—just like any other skill. Once you master it, everything in your life will change for the better." It comes down to this -- if you don't believe in yourself how can someone else?

I had the great pleasure of interviewing Tom Ziglar, the son of Zig Ziglar, and he repeated this famous quote from his father, "You are what you are and you are where you are because of what has gone into your mind. You change what you are and you change where you are by changing what goes into your mind."

If confidence is something you have struggled with in the past, try using the confidence circle activity to help change what goes into your mind. Its purpose is to examine what activities, people and influencers add to and detract from your confidence AND how to go about improving your confidence overtime by taking control over who you spend your time with and what you spend your time doing. The confidence circle is simple, so let me show you how to execute it. Draw 3 circles on a piece of paper

In the innermost circle write the names of people who you consider the closest in your personal and professional life. Then include the activities you do the most (hobbies, TV Shows, movies, podcasts, music, books).

In the 2nd circle, write the names of people you spend a lot of time with and activities you engage with but not quite as much as the inner circle. Now, evaluate the people and activities in the first 2 circles. Think – is this someone or something that contributes to my confidence OR negatively impacts my life? Put a plus sign next to the ones that are positive and a minus sign next to those that are negative.

In the outermost circle, write people who you look up to and content you believe would boost your confidence. Over the next 3 months, invest time and energy moving those people and activities with a + sign closer to the center of your circle and those with a negative to the outside (based on the amount of time you spend with the individual or doing the activity). Just because you move someone or something more to the outside doesn't mean you have to cut them out of your life completely, but limit your time with them and vice versa with positive.

Confidence Circle

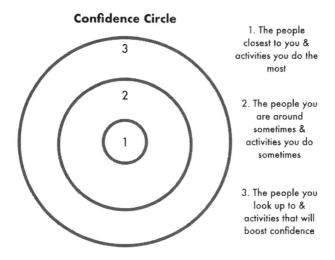

1. The people closest to you & activities you do the most

2. The people you are around sometimes & activities you do sometimes

3. The people you look up to & activities that will boost confidence

Re-do this activity every three months. People and content change over time. You want to evaluate how well you've done at moving those positive people and content into your inner circle.

Drive

The Leadership Compound theory suggests Drive and Confidence tend to go hand-in-hand and most of the time that is true. Drive can be boiled down to motivation. Anyone who's set a goal and failed to reach it knows motivation can be hard to come by.

To quote Zig Ziglar again he said, *"People often say that*

motivation doesn't last. Well, neither does bathing- that's why we recommend it daily."

Here is one simple yet difficult thing you can do to ensure your motivation is in the right place every single day. I learned from entrepreneur, Mac Lackey: Before Mac does anything when he gets to the office, he pulls out a 3x5 notecard and writes WMN on the top. It stands for **What Moves the Needle.** Underneath WMN he writes down one or two things he needs to do that help his organization or team move the needle.

Without deciding proactively what YOU need to get achieved for the good of your organization or team, you run the risk of spending your day doing things that don't matter - things that drain your motivation, but don't move you forward. Before you fire up email or join your first meeting, use a WMN notecard to start your day. You will be motivated to complete the things that matter.

Your WMN card could be a list of tasks to complete, a skill you want to develop, or feedback you want to receive. Make the decision, regardless of how driven you are, to ensure your using your drive to move the needle! You will be shocked at the increase results when you begin working on things that actually matter.

Selflessness

To be selfless means being concerned with the needs and wishes of others, more than your own. But acting selfless isn't easy; it doesn't come naturally to many people.
 Being selfless is a difficult thing to teach, but here are a few ideas you can use:

1. Really listen when other people are talking- I know I sound like a broken record, but listening is a powerful skill people highly underestimate. Make listening a priority.

2. Practice empathy- Put yourself in another person's shoes and think of how they feel. Keep in mind, everyone has their own "stuff" going on. Consider what may be going on in their life or their past experiences. Our past experiences help us create patterns in our behavior which cause us to act and react differently. It's part of what makes everyone so unique, but it can also create a great divide if you're not open to using empathy.

3. Model A Selfless Person- Find someone who exemplifies selfless behavior all the time -- learn from and model their behavior. For me it's the leader of my local Special Olympics chapter.
 Pretty much everything he does is for someone else, and I'm not sure I know a happier and more respected man in the local community.
 Who is this person for you?

Character

Character is defined as the mental and moral qualities distinctive to an individual. It's the behaviors, thoughts, feelings, and actions you exemplify daily. Ultimately, people follow people not titles. So what can you do to build your character?

Try The Mirror Test. Look in the mirror, and ask yourself: Did the thoughts and actions I showed today represent someone I would want to follow? Since this is a self-evaluation test, it means you have to be completely honest. Here are some things to consider when doing the mirror test:

- Did you do what you said you were going to do?
- Did you cut out early or give lackluster effort on a project?
- Did you give importance to the things that really matter professionally?
- Were you humble when good things happen or did you puff up your chest and think it's all about you?

Now, more than ever, people in the workplace are looking for those who exhibit real character. Allow your character to help propel you forward in your leadership journey.

* * *

Take the time to reflect on how you rate in the four areas of the Leadership Compound Theory and note the elements that need your attention.

Rate yourself 1-10 with 1 being the lowest and 10 being the highest for each element:

Confidence   _____

Drive   _____

Selflessness   _____

Character   _____

Where did you rank high and where do you need to put in the work? Take your answers and focus on creating your Leadership Compound.

7

MY DEVELOPMENT

"Leadership is the art of intentional living." -
FARSHAD ASL

Leadership Expert, Marshall Goldsmith, tells a simple
Buddhist story:

*A young farmer paddled his boat vigorously up river.
He was covered with sweat as he paddled his boat
upstream to deliver his produce to the village. It was a
hot day, and he wanted to make his delivery and get
home before dark. As he looked ahead, he spied another
vessel, heading rapidly downstream toward his boat.*

He rowed furiously to get out of the way, but it didn't seem to help.

He shouted, "Change direction! You are going to hit me!" The boat came straight towards him anyway. It hit his boat with a violent thud. The young man cried out, "You idiot! How could you manage to hit my boat in the middle of this wide river?"

As he glared into the boat, seeking out the individual responsible for the accident, he realized that there was no one. He had been screaming at an empty boat that had broken free of its moorings and was floating downstream with the current.

There are too many people with two counterproductive mentalities: "Entitled" and "Victim". Those who are entitled believe their family status, the amount of work they've done, or a list of other bogus reasons, entitles them to results. On the other end of the equation is the victim. They blame others for their challenges – parents, society, teachers, rigged systems, the list could go on and on.

What's interesting is that the victim and the entitled are two sides of the same coin. Neither of them takes responsibility or accountability, but it also means they will never be empowered to take control over their own lives. While there are many issues with these mentalities, the biggest is they breed negativity, a lack of production and enormous hurdle for personal development.

When I first heard Marshall Goldsmith's story of the empty boat, I replayed it three times. I wanted the story to sink in.

So often we are quick to point the blame at someone else. Instead of even worrying about who is at fault, what if you took the idea of the "empty boat" to every situation? How much freedom would you have in your life to move on quickly and respond positively? It's time to no longer blame other people and live the life you are meant to live.

There is a formula for responding intentionally to events. I learned this formula from leadership expert Tim Kight, the Founder of Focus 3: E + R = O

Event
+ Response
Outcome

This is a powerful formula that puts YOU in control and

requires you to take full personal responsibility for the outcome of any event or situation you encounter. No more entitlement, victimization, blaming others, luck, karma, the universe, fate, or whatever else you use to deflect blame. You can learn more about the formula at focus3.com.

So what does all this have to do with leadership and moving up in your career? In order for you to achieve more favorable outcomes, you have to be intentional with everything from your actions at work, at home and your personal development as a human being. In order for you to better grasp this idea of intentionality there is something called the Circle of Intentionality.

Circle of Intentionality

Let me explain. The circle of intentionality creates a barrier between your comfort zone and being intentional. Ultimately just like the empty boat, you get to decide your response and if you are in or out of the circle – in or outside of your comfort zone. When you are intentional with your actions and development, you stretch yourself to step outside of the circle. You're thinking about how your reaction to events or choices you make will impact the outcome for you and for others. You're being thoughtful with your actions and your words and the meaning behind them.

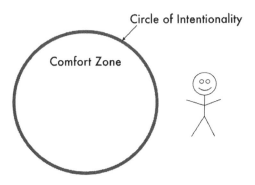

When you stay in the circle, you are limited to how much you can achieve and grow. You live life comfortably, on auto-pilot, thinking about number one. It's not until you step outside the circle that you create a world of positive outcomes and opportunities. The best part is, the longer you practice and master intentionality the smaller your circle (comfort zone) will become which makes being intentional easier.

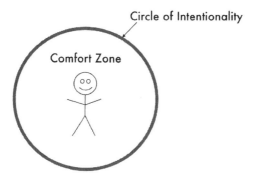

My friend, Rachel, is a perfect example of intentionality at work. She had just received word that she was passed over for a big promotion. The company promoted a man that she felt she deserved the job over. Instead of responding emotionally by staying inside her comfort zone, she stepped outside of the circle and thought about the bigger picture. She approached her leader the next day with a level head and simply asked for an explanation of the decision and voiced her disappointment. This type of approach allowed her leader to fully explain the rationale behind the decision and why it was made. It turns out the other candidate made his desire to move up and lead others to a clear professional goal from day one. This person's intentionality was the only difference between Rachel and the man who received the promotion . The feedback was eye-opening. She went on to get multiple promotions at the company over the next few years, but none of it would have been possible if she would have responded inside the circle of intentionality by immediately voicing her initial anger and assumptions of sexism. In doing so, she risked the possibility of being let go and burning bridges to future career opportunities.

Putting it into Practice

Our days are filled with events. Our research has shown as many as 500 events occur in a normal workday. Regardless of how small or how big the event is, the important thing is to remember is the formula:

EVENT + RESPONSE = OUTCOME

So how do you go about being intentional with your response 500+ times in day? We have a 3-step process to help you be more intentional with your response to drive positive outcomes.

Step 1. Stop.
Take a deep breath. If needed, remove yourself from the situation to get your mind right. It can be as simple as saying, "I need time to think this over before I get back to you."

Step 2. Reflect.

Ask yourself:

What is my initial thought?

Who will be impacted in the outcome?

What would the outcome be if I reacted in that way?

What positive outcome do I want?

How can I react to achieve that positive outcome?

WARNING: this is not about playing out a million "what if" situations and "what if-ing" yourself into non-action. This shouldn't be based on FEAR, but instead on achieving a positive outcome.

Step 3. React.

Put together your response and be confident when delivering it. It seems simple, but it's especially difficult if you've been staying within the circle of intentionality.

Being Proactively Intentional

There's a difference between reacting to an event and being proactively intentional with your words and actions. These are the things you can proactively, to help separate yourself as a leader in your organization and in life.

Be Relentless in your Professional Development

Mike Watt famously said, "I wanna try and stay a student for life." Watt's musical career spans decades and for good reason. If you are unrelenting in your development as a professional, you almost have zero chance of failing. You will always be valuable to an organization if you're an expert in your field. Every week on the *Follow My Lead* Podcast I ask our guest a simple question, "What's the best investment you have ever made?" 90% of time the answer is, "Without question, it's the investment I made in myself." Traditionally, you may believe your education is the biggest investment you can make, but learning doesn't end with a degree. The leaders I've interviewed spoke about reading, listening to and watching content that adds to their knowledge base and keeps them at the forefront of their industry. Make an effort to invest in yourself – whether it's just time or time and money to continue your education beyond what's required of you.

Serve Others

One of my favorite quotes ever comes from Dr. Martin Luther King Jr. He said, "Life's most important and urgent question is, 'What are you doing for others?'" Possessing a servant heart, not a selfish heart is a truly proactive exercise. You can serve others in many ways at work – stay late to help complete a project or bring coffee or bagels to the office for breakfast. Keep your eyes and ears open to the struggles and needs of those around you and look for ways to help. More importantly, do it proactively, without hesitation.

Serving outside of work is just as essential. You can do things like volunteering at a non-profit organization to serve a cause you are passionate about or giving time or money to a cause that's important to you. Non-profits may be in need of people to volunteer their professional skills as well. For example, accounting or video production services. Only you can decide what works for you and how you want serve — the key is that you are helping others. If you do these service-oriented things for the right reason there is no chance they go unnoticed.

Align Goals to Win/Win

Mark came to me one day and said, "I want to learn how to code." When I asked him why, he said, "My goal is to learn how to code so I can help further develop our software product." By making his goal our team's goal, he became increasingly more valuable to the team. We made time in his schedule to devote to the development of his software development skills, and Mark was awarded a pay raise once he used them in them in the workplace.

Align your personal goals and your team's goals. Achieving goals becomes powerful when they benefit a larger organizational cause. Whatever your goals are and I know you have them, the key is to align your short-term goals to the goals of your organization or team.

Get Advocates

The definition of an advocate is a person who publicly supports or recommends a cause (or in our case an individual). If a mentor or colleague got promoted would they want you on their new team? Would they put their reputation on the line for you? If the answers are yes, you've got yourself an advocate.

Advocates are more than just people who will get you promoted. When seeking out advocates, keep in mind, it's a two-way street. You want people who will help you grow, look out for you, and pull you up. But you should also offer value to them as well.

Getting advocates isn't as simple as asking, "Will you advocate for me?" You must build relationships overtime. There are a lot of ways to do this but it starts with asking to have a conversation. Find out what their goals are and where they need help. Ask to have coffee, lunch or a more extended meeting to learn about their professional journey. Then you can uncover ways to create a mutually beneficial relationship. Again, it starts with you intentionally listening to them and then adding value first. After you've solidified a relationship over time, you can move from acquaintance to advocate. Here's a warning: If you're only out for number one, you won't be fooling anyone.

Manage Up

Bob Beaudine a friend and author of *The Power of Who* said, "If you can't communicate your goals and dreams with the closest people to you, how are they going to know how to help you?" Managing up is a method of career development that's based on the mutual benefit of yourself and your leader.

Awareness is the first step. Intentionally and purposefully letting others know your goals and committing your actions to achieving those goals is a perfect way to manage up. It's not about manipulating or being pushy. Instead, just communicate your vision or goals and so your leader can be looking for opportunities or projects that could help you get there. Remember my friend, Rachel? If she would have communicated her goals to her manager, she may have won the promotion over the other candidate.

Are you leaving projects, opportunities or promotions to complete chance? You are, if you haven't communicated your goals with your leader so they can help you.

Every time I talk about managing up, I always hear,

"Well, my manager wouldn't want to promote me." My answer is simple, "If you have never communicated your desires to your leader, how do you know for sure? The worst they can do is respond negatively. Then you will know you are working for the wrong leader." Sometimes, we let our own negative self-talk stand in the way of our success. But know, it's the responsibility of a leader to develop more leaders, not more followers.

I am not under any dissolution that implementing anything in this step in the F.M.L. framework is easy. It's without question the hardest thing for professionals to get right because it not only deals with being intentional with your motives and actions at work, but also your response to events out of your control. Like with anything that's challenging, there are rewards for those who commit and achieve.

At the end of the day better people make better leaders. It's all about the journey of oneself and then the impact that self has on others. You can become more like this on an ongoing basis if you are committed to your development as a professional. Keep in mind you will continue to meet people throughout your life who will make you want to continue to improve and further your development, so your development will never be complete.

8

LEAD BY EXAMPLE

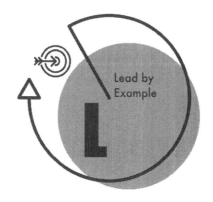

"The most powerful leadership tool you have is your own personal example" – JOHN WOODEN

Barry Bonds played 22 seasons in Major League Baseball, was a 14 time all-star, holds the all-time home run mark for a career (762), holds the record for most home runs in a season (73), and yet he isn't in the Baseball Hall of Fame. Now if you know anything about his story you probably know he has been linked to many reports of Performance Enhancing Drugs (PED's) which is why even with all his great accomplishments, the people who vote for the Baseball Hall of Fame have not elected him. The questionable decisions he made off the baseball field derailed his dream of becoming a Hall of Famer. Whether Bonds did or didn't use PED's isn't the point. The point is the perception of Bonds is that he was a cheater and there is almost nothing he can do now to change that perception and get into the Baseball Hall of Fame.

Just like Bonds, the decisions and actions you make every single day as a professional at work absolutely dictate your perception. It doesn't matter if you are the CEO or an entry-level employee, your example matters.

Take Jill for example. It could have been her untimely arrival at the office on a regular basis, the bolting out the door the minute the clock struck 5:30pm, the constant distraction of looking at her cell phone, the general lack of enthusiasm about her teammates, or the constant distractions she made during the day. The entire team was growing tired of Jill's demeanor.

But this isn't just Jill's story. I bet if you stopped for a second, you could probably switch Jill's name for a few colleagues. What's worse, is you might put yourself in this scenario. This type of behavior is a major problem in work environments. Too many are people completely unaware of the example they demonstrate through their actions and how it effects the outcome of their career.

* * *

Most people can directly relate to the desire to have a boss who leads by example. Think about it:

- Do you like to be told to stay at the office until 6:00pm when the boss leaves early every day?
- Do you like to be told you have 14 days paid vacation a year when the boss takes 45?
- Do you like to be told the importance of having a good attitude when the boss walks in grumpy and negative every day?

Of course you don't like or want any of these scenarios because people like a leader who leads by example. You want a leader who is willing to put in the work and lives up to the same standard to which they hold you accountable.

The Perception Predicament

"Life is all about perception. Positive versus negative. Whichever you choose will affect and more than likely reflect your outcome" - Sonya Declai

We had called every single person in both our phones to come babysit on Thursday night and had struck out 20 times. No one could pull through for us. Just about that time my wife said, "I have one last option. A friend of mine gave me this girl's name and number months ago but I've never used her." Instead of immediately calling her, I suggested we do a little digging on social media prior to letting her keep our kids. It didn't take long to see pictures and videos of her partying, drinking, and being immature. Within minutes we had made our decision. Even though we desperately needed a babysitter, this girl wasn't going to get a call from us.

Our perception of the girl became a reality once we did our research. We let the visuals she chose to share on social media create a story about her that effected our decision not to hire her.

The moral of the story is the example you set creates other people's perception of you. Let me repeat this because it's so important. Your actions and behavior play a massive part in the perception others have of you. Whether you like it or not perception often times becomes a reality. So being perceived as a leader is the key to becoming one.

How people perceive you is broken into what we call the 5 P's of Perception:

* * *

5 P's of Perception

Presence Online

What's the first thing I do when I have a meeting scheduled with someone? I look at their social profile. It's your resume, your calling card, it's your identity. It's where people engage with each other today. So everything that you show [profile], share [updates], and engage with [comment] matters. And yes, includes things that you think "disappear" forever. Want proof? Google D'angelo Russell SnapChat and you'll see what I'm talking about.

So the question you have to ask yourself is: Does your online presence portray you as a leader? There are three critical areas to focus on to ensure your online presence provides a positive perception:

1. **Profile**. The most popular professional network today is LinkedIn. Ensure your profile picture is professional and your description accurately defines what you do, not just your current job title. On more personal networks like Facebook or Instagram it is just as important to present yourself in a way that shows you have matured past the point of being a social butterfly. Consider how you want others to perceive you and choose what you share carefully. Whether we like it or not, most people do judge a (face)book by its cover photo.

2. **Updates.** For the sake of including all social networks and platforms, updates are considered what you upload, share, or even "like". Every picture, Tweet, Snapchat, and post is important. One bad move can ruin your perception for a long time. One of the most powerful tests you can use when considering your actions online is simply asking yourself, "If one of my organizational leaders posted this, what would I think?" If you have any doubt at all about whether it's a good idea to share a particular update, I would lean to the side of caution and pass on hitting the share button.

3. **Comments.** Engaging in conversation online is a powerful way to stand out and get people to remember you. Unfortunately your comments

can also have as much a negative effect as a positive one. Keep comments positive, encouraging, and cordial. You are allowed to disagree, but your response should be conducive to a positive discussion. In other words, don't be a troll. As a test, ask yourself, "Would I say this in front of my mother?" Or even "Would I say this to someone in-person?"

Professionalism

Each company's culture is different, but being a professional is consistent across the board. It's about aligning to your company's culture. How you dress, communication mediums you use and your work ethic all matter. Alignment to company culture comes in many forms. Here are two key areas to focus on to stand out in a positive way:

1. **Dress Code.** Sam Ramsey famously said, "Dress for the job you want, not the one you have." Be intentional about dressing for the job you want. Take for example a young professional who likes to wear business casual to work. In a less formal environment his dress code would make him stand out. Yet in a more formal environment it makes him look dressed-down or maybe even out of place. This is just a case of observing and taking cues from your

surroundings. You don't have to worry about wearing certain brands or spending thousands of dollars on new clothes, but your appearance should be polished. You'd be surprised in someone's perception of the difference between a crisp ironed shirt and pair of slacks vs. jeans and a t-shirt. If there's one take away I want you to remember, "Look the Part."

2. **Communication.** In most corporate environments email is the preferred mechanism for communication. If that's the case, write clear, concise emails with good grammar and subject lines that communicate what needs to be accomplished. Always reread your email twice prior to hitting send. If you read them out loud, often times it's easy to catch mistakes or simplify the message. If your organization's communication medium is less formal, apply the same principles. Always re-read messages before hitting send, because it's the little things that matter. Note: you can use these same ideas for polishing your online presence. There's nothing worse than a glaring typo on something as important as your LinkedIn page.

Positivity

No one likes a negative Nancy or a Debbie downer.
 Being positive doesn't mean you have to turn a blind eye

to what's happening around you. It's all-too-common in the workplace for people to have a negative attitude or mindset. By having a positive and optimistic attitude you will not only be more pleasant to be around but you will stand out. There are four simple things you can do to be more positive:

1. **Appreciate the opportunity you have.** Give thanks both verbally and through your actions to those who provided you the opportunity. An occasional thank you note or text message is never a bad idea.

2. **Avoid negative individuals or groups.** Provide positive comments and don't engage in negative feedback when they happen. It can be difficult not to give into the conversation, but once those around you see you bring an optimistic outlook, it will wear off on them.

3. **Display enthusiasm**. Enthusiasm is contagious. If you're going to spend eight hours or more a day at work, why not make it more than just tolerable? Make an effort to smile, laugh, and enjoy your job.

4. **Practice random acts of kindness.** Each day try to do something kind and helpful. Volunteer for a project, or if you run an errand ask if anyone needs anything, or give someone a compliment. You don't have to do anything

elaborate, just keep your eyes out for opportunities to do a good deed.

Passion

Most people think of passion as doing what you love – which by itself is fine. But passion in the context of the 5 P's is being passionate about your company, the industry, the people, and the products and services you offer your customers. Being passionate can be an enormous differentiator over people who just show up to punch the proverbial clock. Typically the more you know, the better you become at your job, and the more passion you will have.

There aren't many tricks for how to create this passion, but devouring company marketing materials and publications by thought leaders in your industry are great ways to start developing this passion.

Proactivity

Proactivity is the hardest of the P's – but quite possibly the most coveted and the one that will create the most differentiation for you (and one we've touched on earlier in the book). Do you do things to help your leader, team or organization advance -- without being told to do so? It literally can change the trajectory of your career. Proactivity one can be tricky because it requires you to take chances, ignore the "what-ifs" to move beyond the status quo. It's a leap of faith in yourself – to take action, not knowing for certain what the results will be. It's a mix of hustling and being a relentless problem solver. Here is a 5 step process to be more proactive:

1. **Know only you can do it**. No one else can get you where you want to go, not your parents, your boss, or your colleagues. Once you grasp this, you can begin to truly start the proactive process.

2. **Look for problems**. Look at your normal workflow, and see if you can identify problems that keep occurring. These problems are now opportunities to be proactive.

3. **Identify Solutions.** Now you can look for solutions to proactively eliminate those problems you uncovered. Sometimes finding solutions to problems takes trial and error, but with tenacity, you will break through with a solution.

4. **Show Accountability.** Hold yourself accountable to the process of looking for problems and solutions. Start by writing down 2 or 3 problems a week and brainstorm solution ideas for 30 minutes a day.

5. **Celebrate Successes**. One way to stay proactive is to celebrate your wins.

Remember, perception equals reality. If you put the 5 P's

of Perception: Presence Online, Professionalism, Positivity, Passion, and Proactivity in action every single day by your example you will create a positive perception. I can assure you, leading by example, will have others wanting to follow you.

PART 3

THAT WAS JUST THE BEGINNING

9

GOING BEYOND
EXPECTATIONS

"Don't lower your expectations to meet your performance. Raise your level of performance to meet your expectations." - RALPH MARSTON

Steve was one of the best performers any leader could ask for. I wasn't afraid to push him to the limit and hold him to a high standard. One day I sensed things were off with Steve. I called him into my office and said, "I have been watching you closely for the last few weeks and I see a problem emerging. Steve, have you ever heard of the 10-70-20 principle of employee performance?" He said, "no." I then approached the whiteboard and said, "The principle says that every organization consists of three groups. Let me explain with a graph. On the Y-axis, is 'performance' and the X-axis is 'time at the organization'. There is a line that travels from left to right that represents what your hired measured or fired to do – better-known as: what your organization expects from you -- most people I have come across have no clue this line even exists. They work and work and work but don't have a good sense of this line."

"Let's take you for example. When you were first hired, the expectations started pretty low, to allow you to get up to speed on our business and industry. But over a few weeks or a month the line began to increase much like we want a stock market graph to look, just a steady incline of growth. Then at some point my expectations level off for you – with only slight increases over a long period of time, as you learn new skills, your tenure increases, or the industry changes."

10-70-20 PRINCIPLE

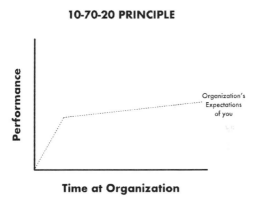

Time at Organization

I continued, "10% of people will never quite reach the organization's expectation – these people are the ones who get their desk moved, until they find themselves in the basement looking for their red stapler before they're fired from the company."

10-70-20 PRINCIPLE

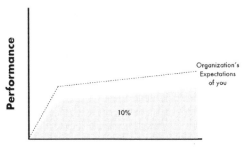

"There's a magic point on this line – at one year where most people (the 70%) hit a proficiency level. Some years may be a little better or a little worse, but most people map right at or near their expectation-level.

10-70-20 PRINCIPLE

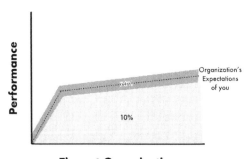

"Then, you have the last 20%. These are the people who not only reach expectation, but then exceed it, year over year. They're disciplined, driven, self-motivated and work relentlessly to reach higher-levels of performance. These are people who have the ability to not only achieve great things but also to become great leaders.

10-70-20 PRINCIPLE

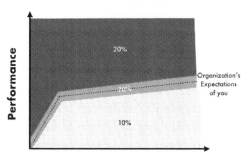

Since I know you are into football think of someone like Tom Brady, the surefire Hall of Fame quarterback of the New England Patriots. He has continued to get better every single year of his career. His age isn't even catching up to him. In the 2016 season at the age of 39 he threw 28 touchdowns and had only 2 interceptions all season! He quite possible is the best quarterback in history with 5 Super Bowl wins under his belt. Tom could have been like many people at the top who flatlined, but he takes a personal challenge at the beginning of every year to get better. He devotes himself to his mind, body and soul to ensure he improves and exceeds expectations."

"Everyone in the top 20% is susceptible to becoming victims of comfort and can flatline at any point in their career, but still remaining above the expectation line. Comfort is the enemy of personal and professional growth. In fact: Comfort = Minimum Growth."

I continued in the conversation , "Tom Brady never got comfortable. In fact he was uncomfortable with being comfortable. He takes care of his body like no other quarterback in history, he practices and puts in work well beyond what most people need to". Steve, I have seen your flatline trending these last few weeks.. The challenge for you will be to maintain a constant level of hustle and dedication for personal and professional growth like Tom Brady. I'm not under the false impression that this will be easy. In fact I am more than aware this is difficult. But as I have said to you since day one, 'If it was easy... everyone would do it.'"

Steve sat up a little straighter in his chair, and said, "Thank you, I understand and I can take it from here, it's the only way forward."

Over the next 6 months, Steve took our conversation to heart and put it into action. Amazing things began to happen that produced phenomenal results. Instead of being stuck in concrete, he was moving at warp speed.

So the next time you think you have hit a ceiling or are stuck in slow motion, think about the 10-70-20 principle and proactively evaluate your actions and begin doing things that challenge you. At times these moments or events can be painful, but keep in mind the things that test and challenge you are where you'll find the greatest reward.

Where the 20% Excel

In our research, we've found that there are 4 areas where the upper 20% really excel. Some of these are little things, but they make a huge impact on your performance – and promotion decisions of your organization. If you can model these behaviors, you'll be exceeding expectation in no time.

Productivity

Professionals can stand out just by getting things done quickly and effectively. If that takes getting to work early, staying late, working on weekends or just grinding when you are in the office, make it happen. Productivity is about using your time wisely and not wasting other' time as well. I immediately think to an example of 4 young professionals on a conference call. Instead of taking notes, engaging in the conversation, and adding value, they were all on their phones surfing Instagram until it was their time to speak. This is the opposite of taking productivity seriously and unfortunately it is way more common than the alternative in today's business environment.

Communication

A friend of mine named, Doug LaBrosse is a financial advisor and a master of communication. Being one of the youngest advisors in his firm, Doug knows one of the primary ways he can differentiate himself over other advisors is to take time where others might drop the ball. He clearly communicates recaps of conversations with colleagues as well as current and prospective clients. He leaves no stone unturned with it comes to his communication. His emails are professional, well thought out, and timely. Doug knows clear communication is an extension of his brand and business. How well you communicate will makes a huge difference in your career. Think of the three keys of communication to improve:

1. How often
2. How succinct
3. How well you maximize your time

Results

Don't forget for one second why your organization pays you. It isn't because they have to, it's because they expect results and a return on their financial investment on you. Regardless of your role, your performance and the results you achieve impact what others think about you and your career. You can be the smartest person in the room, but if you're not doing something that helps drive the bottom line, your value quickly depletes. If you are in sales, hitting and exceeding quota is how you're measured. Crush the quota. If you are in customer service, having positive feedback from clients is critical. Don't let a customer hang up without asking them to provide feedback to your manager about the service you provided. Measure your performance based on the results, not feelings. If you don't have a defined way to measure your performance, ask your managers to help you define one so you can measure against it.

Expertise

Tim Sullivan is an expert in the world of sales methodologies and sales performance. In some ways he might be one of the top 10 people in the world on this subject. Tim didn't gain this level of expertise by just going through the motions at work. He is an avid reader, writer, and student of his profession. The best part is there is no limit or age restriction on how well a professional knows their industry or job. The only restriction is how much effort people put into gaining the expertise. Some simple questions to evaluate your expertise:

1. Could you teach others about your business?
2. Do you know on the state of your market and industry?
3. Do you have an educated opinion where it's going?

These four areas: productivity, communication, results, and expertise are where the top 20% of the 10-70-20 excel. Here is the kicker that is so important:, they are all measurable. They are often used as quantifiable evidence when it comes to offering promotions and leadership positions. I can't overstate their direct correlation to your ability to move up and excel in your organization.

So, as you move forward on your path towards becoming a leader, keep the 10-70-20 principle in mind and never fall victim to comfort.

10

THERE IS NO 'I' TEAM

"Individually, we are one drop. Together, we are an ocean." - **RYUNOSUKE SANTORO**

Leicester City started the 2015 season as a 5000 to 1 underdog to win the English Premier League. To give you a perspective, those are the same odds some bookmakers give to Elvis still being alive. Needless to say, they weren't expected to have a good season by the experts. The previous season they finished 14th out of 20 teams and they had lost a few of their best players to free agency. The team had a payroll of 54.4 million Pounds -- the same amount rival Manchester City spent on a single player.

Claudio Raneiri ,their manager, was on the hot seat coming into the season but in his heart he knew this team was different. In his 30-year coaching career he had never seen a team like this. A team that played for each other and not the other way around. They played as a unit instead as individuals and they formed a bond of teamwork that carried them to win the 2015 English Premier League title as a 5000 to 1 underdog. The longest shot to win any team title in the history of world sports and the game wasn't even close. There are many theories as to why this team was so special, and what they did to make it happen, but when you net it out it's simple. They lifted each other and collectively create greatness.

The ability for any one person to do remarkable things hinges on how well they can make those around them better.

To further make the point, the MVP of the English primer league that year, Jamie Vardy, was none other than a player on Leicester City,. He was purchased by the team in 2012 for 1 million Pounds, cheap by league standards. Jamie had a history of individual success over his career, but without the team winning, the championship was an honor he never would have received.

Consider this point., The more you think of your role as lifting the team, the better your odds of professional success. I love to explain it to people with the Pencil Theory. If you hold one #2 pencil, it is fairly easy to break. However, if you 5 pencils together and try to break them, it is nearly impossible. The stronger you can make the bond between your team members, the harder it will be to break the team, and the easier it will be for the collective group to have success.

One of the most important lessons in this book is the need to change your mindset from "my" professional progression to "our" progression. I don't pretend this is an easy mindset to achieve particularly early in your career, but there is a reason why professional athletes covet team championship over individual awards.

When It's All About You

What good is all the money in the world if all you have it for is to spend it on yourself? Eventually you run out of material things to buy. What good is having a mansion if you go home to an empty house overnight? Eventually you get lonely. What good is all the achievement in the world without others to celebrate it with? Eventually you will get discouraged looking in the mirror giving yourself a smile and an imaginary fist pump.

In 2013 I was given an individual sales award in front of the entire company and all of their significant others at an annual Christmas party. As I approached the CEO to shake his hand, he asked me to say a few words to the group. Since I was unaware that I would win the award, I hadn't prepared a speech. As I turned to the microphone, I looked out at all the people who had helped make this possible and the only words I could come up with was "thank you." It was probably the easiest thing to say, because it was so true. I mentioned ten or more people that I knew with 100% certainty had made this moment possible for me.

Looking back on it, if I had taken the microphone and only boasted about all the work I had put in, I would have done a major disservice to the company. The lesson is simple: The only way you make it, is by the help of others and working as a team.

So take the old adage "there is no 'I' in team" and live by it every single day of your career. Sure there will be times when you have to make decisions based on the good of you and your family, but those big decisions will not be possible without your mindset being "we" instead of "I."

How can you get this mindset shift from "I" to "We" to become a habit?

Don't go one day at the office without asking a colleague if there is anything you you can do to help and then give some more. I mean give until it's a sacrifice.

Offering vs Sacrifice

Toussaint Romain received national press by CNN, Fox News, and a slew of other outlets for the role he played in the September 2016 riots in Charlotte, NC. For 3 nights the city of Charlotte had enormous protests for the police killing of an African American man named Keith Lamont Scott. For multiple days the local and national papers showed pictures of police in full-on riot gear fending off crowds of angry citizens. In the middle of the police and the citizens stood an African American man in a tie named Toussaint Romain. I sat down with Toussaint months later to interview him about leadership and the role all Americans should play in bridging the growing racial divide in the United States. As the conversation progressed, I asked Toussaint about the idea of offering vs. sacrifice and he told this story:

Mr. Hog lived on a farm. One day Mr. Farmer got sick and couldn't do anything. Mrs. Farmer got tired because she was trying to take care of Mr. Farmer and the farm. Together they laid on their bed, sick and tired. The animals, who were fed day in and day out, hadn't been fed in three days. So the animals gathered together in the red barn. They sent one of the pigeons up to look into Mr. and Mrs. Farmer's window and check on them. He saw them lying in bed and flew back down to report to the other animals. He said, "Listen everybody, they're lying in bed, not moving. They must be sick and tired." The animals talked among themselves, "Mr. and Mrs. Farmer are always taking things from us and they eat it. I think it's called breakfast." So they asked the chickens for some eggs. The horses were asked to gather apples and oranges from the trees. They asked the cows to give some milk. Together, they gathered the food and they began up the path to the house. On their way, they pass by Mr. Hog's pen. He's rolling around in the mud. "Mr. Hog! Mr. Hog! We need you to help us out!" The animals cried, "Mr. and Mrs. Farmer are sick and tired so we're giving them breakfast. Everyone is giving their part. We need you to give your part, too. We need you to give us bacon." Mr. Hog ignores them. "Mr. Hog, stop being lazy," the animals shouted, "give us some bacon."

Mr. Hog turns back to them and says, "Listen, for you to give eggs and milk is nice. It's an offering. But for me to give bacon is a sacrifice...because it means I must die."

The moral of the story is giving a sacrifice is hard, but we are all called to sacrifice. It's easy for a rich person to give an offering of money from one's abundance. It's easy for someone with no job to give an offering of their time. Now I am not suggesting you have to die for your colleagues, but I am suggesting you think about what you can sacrifice for the good of the team or company. What I have found is the people who are willing to sacrifice something to help a team be successful always rise to the top. It could be as simple as bypassing a few weekends of going out with friends to stay home and learn a new skill to help the team fill a void. Think back to my colleague who proactively chose to learn to code. This isn't something he had to do and he has given up nights and weekends to develop a skill we desperately needed. It could be staying late to help a new young team member. Helping them learn the ropes outside of working hours will get your team at 100% capacity and will help everyone. It could be volunteering to mentor young students or underprivileged kids to improve your local community.

The key here is you figure out what would be difficult for you to do or painful at first glance and decide to do it anyways to help others. The minute you start sacrificing is the first sign you truly believe there is no "I" in team. I promise your personal and professional life will be richer and more rewarding when you make sacrifices.

11

MOUSETRAPS

"Be About Actions, Not Distractions" - UNKNOWN

One afternoon earlier this year, I sat down to write my weekly leadership blog for LinkedIn. I soon found myself stuck in the first paragraph grasping for words to fill the page. I knew the topic I was writing about, I knew the content, but I couldn't seem to muster more than a few sentences.

Instead of powering through a small case of writer's block, I opened up my web browser and scrolled through all the pages I typically check during the workday –I checked website statistics, LinkedIn, and podcast traffic. I must admit I also fell for one click bait headline, "How to be a better writer in 10 minutes." Once I ran out of web pages, I turned to my cell phone and opened Instagram to check 'likes' on my latest post. Once I exhausted Instagram, I opened Facebook to do the same. Before I knew it, I was interrupted by my next meeting reminder. It was like the notification was meant to hit me between the eyes and instead of saying "client call at 4:00pm" it should have said, "You just wasted one hour of your life and got absolutely nothing accomplished."

I quickly realized these distractions were nothing more than mousetraps. As great as technology can be, much of it is actually designed to be a mousetrap. Mousetraps are things created by others to create distractions in our lives that move us away from doing work that matters. Until I realized these distractions were actually mousetraps, they were going to continue to hurt me. I proactively decided to either remove them or create defenses against them.

So what are the most common mousetraps that will derail your progress as a professional and what can you do to proactively remove or create defenses against them?

Cell Phone

What do you do when you are bored? You pull that phone out of your pocket and find something, anything to stop the boredom. It doesn't matter if it's scrolling social networks, texting a friend or playing a game -- anything will do. Unfortunately this is an absolute productivity killer at work. It takes you away from things you could or should be doing to wasting time for the sake of a bad habit. If that wasn't bad enough, we have become so attached to our phone that it affects our relationships at work and at home. We send an awful 'message,' to the people sitting in front of us by pulling our phones out to glance at them.

I wish I had a perfect solution for this problem, as I am as guilty as any, but I do know that no problem is solved without first admitting it's a problem. Some of the best remedies I have found are putting my cell phone in a desk drawer at work and checking it at certain times of the day or going upstairs to plug it in when I get home so it doesn't distract time with my family.

Facebook

There is absolutely nothing wrong with Facebook conceptually. It's a wonderful social platform to reconnect with old friends and stay up to date on the major events happening in the world. And it's turned into an incredible marketing tool for businesses. The problem is, it's addicting and can create bad habits as well. So if you are like most people, you probably open the app on your phone a few times a day. Research shows the average person spends 27 hours a month on Facebook and nearly 22 of those are on the mobile application. I ran a two-week test a year ago by deleting the Facebook app from my phone, but not banning myself from the platform completely. What happened was amazing. I found myself not even wanting to check it regularly because the desktop experience wasn't as good as mobile. I ended up with 3 clear benefits to this experiment: decreased wasted time, learning more, and I had more positive mental thoughts because I wasn't looking at "the best moments" of everyone else's lives.

Colleague Chitchat

You probably have a couple offenders in your office. They stop by your desk to chat about the weekend or to tell a story that has nothing to do with work. It's commonplace in the office. While like the other mousetraps there is nothing inherently wrong with building relationships with coworkers, it does take you away from being productive. If you are anything like me, it then takes 5 or 10 additional minutes to get back in the groove. If you really start to watch this around the office, you will find the most productive people don't engage in a lot of chit chat. Sure they stop and say hello or ask about the weekend on a Monday morning, but they don't engage in lengthy discussions.

If you often fall victim to office chitchat, it's completely acceptable to say to a colleague, "I would love to hear all about it, but I am working on something right now. Can we talk about it at lunch or when we are walking out after work?" You will be pleasantly surprised by how easily people accept your response without taking offense.

I couldn't even begin to mention all of the mousetraps

that exist and you will certainly have different ones than your colleagues or me. If you can just channel your inner focus and proactively decide that you are going to take control of the situation, you will without question avoid the mousetraps in your life.

12

PERMISSION GRANTED

"It's easier to ask for forgiveness than it is to get permission" - UNKNOWN

As Kevin Nussbaum looked up from behind the wall of his cube, I could see something in his eyes that I had not yet seen from him. It was a look of determination and a person ready for action. To give you a little background , he is a military veteran and is now manning his post as an IT professional in a mid-size company. He is well-liked and always brings a positive attitude to the office.

Kevin was preparing to unleash a 21-day, 10,000 step challenge. He started to gauge the interest of others in the office. Once he had enough interest from 5-10 people, he made it a team event to build camaraderie. All of a sudden what began with a few people turned into the entire global company getting involved and making teams. Almost 90% of the company's employees participated.

It started with one man in IT and created a buzz around the company that couldn't have been created by the CEO, even if he tried. The health benefits were phenomenal as everyone collectively walked a quarter of the way around the earth!

Who knew a small idea like this could create such a great impact on an organization and its culture? Kevin didn't need permission to lead. He chose to lead. He didn't wait for his title to change to CTO or Head of IT to positively impact his company. Every single professional in the world has the same ability to create positive change in their organization because leadership is about the first 4 letters of the word. L-E-A-D. Lead is a verb. It's about action and it's everyone's job to figure out what actions to take and put them into motion."

In many ways, the corporate leadership system is broken. Employees are frustrated by layer upon layer of management that communicates poorly, lacks a business purpose, and has a larger concern for the almighty dollar than the people who produce it. These problems and challenges aren't new, but the insurgence of the Millennial and Gen Z generations has created an urgency for change. Professionals want big changes to occur, but don't know where to start. I believe it begins with this idea of choosing to lead.

Truth be told, what this world needs now more than ever is: More Leaders, Not Less.

* * *

It needs people who lead from the front lines – people who don't wait for their boss to give them permission to lead.   Here are some things you can do immediately to begin your pursuit of leading today regardless of what role you are in:

Don't Forget the Meaning of Leadership

Think back to the beginning of this book and John Adams' definition of leadership, "If your actions inspire people to dream more, learn more, do more, and become more you are a leader."

Leadership isn't about the title you hold because people follow people, not titles. Once you understand this and take it to heart, you won't care about what your title is, you will care about impacting other people in a positive way. Regardless of how quick your rise is up the ranks in your organization, it's so important not to forget the true purpose of Leadership.

In the Bible , Peter denied Jesus three times. But before that, he told Jesus he would never in a million years deny him. Yet, sure enough he did. I don't care if you have to print out Adams' definition of leadership and keep it visible for you to see at all times, the key is for you to do whatever it takes to remember it.

Control what you can control

Every single day you have control over your attitude, effort and enthusiasm. When you wake up in the morning these three things will dictate your day. It's so easy to let the first 30 or 45 minutes of our day dictate our attitude, effort and enthusiasm for the entire day. It could be the emails that came in overnight, a disagreement with a spouse, a baby crying or a bad hair day. The event really isn't important. What is important is your response. Remember the equation Event + Response = Outcome? You control your response to events and the more you begin to buy into that notion and put it into practice, the better your odds of controlling your attitude, effort and enthusiasm.

Have a sense of urgency

No one is guaranteed a tomorrow. Our lives at home and at work move fast. Months fly by like weeks, quarters happen like months and years pass by before we even know it. One of the most common things I hear from mentors whose children are now adults, is "cherish the time you have with your kids, it goes by so fast." And for anyone who doesn't have kids and can't relate, just think back to your high school or college years. Looking back, the time flew by, even though in the moment, time seemed to drag on forever.

Brent Musburger, the famous sportscaster announced

his retirement from live television in 2017 after over forty years in the business. His last comment before signing off for good was, "It's such a short time span from your first job until social security. Make the most of it." Think about that for a second. Someone who saw and called thousands of games from the best seat in the house felt his career flew by. Having a sense of urgency to enjoy the moment and completely be present in each and every job is critical to not only achieve your potential, but to enjoy life.

I have a sense of urgency about spending quality time with my kids because I know how fast it's going to go. I have come to believe waiting for someone else to tell you what to do or waiting for direction is one of the worst habits you can fall into. Urgency is a mindset, it's being ready to go the minute you walk in the door of your office. Urgency is a habit that every professional can develop, maintain, and use to hold others accountable.

Get small wins daily

One of the most popular remarks I hear from modern professionals is, "I don't know how to get started" or "everything is being done, so there is nothing for me to do here." My answer is always the same, "find anything that will get you a small win." It doesn't matter how big or small it may be, because getting small wins every single day turns into something bigger over time.

If you had to cut down a big oak tree with a single ax how would you cut it down? The only way is to hit it the same spot every day and over time you will do some real damage. Eventually, the tree will fall. It's the small wins that add up --starting a 10,000 step challenge, formulating a purpose statement, mentoring new employees or having a sense of urgency. What matters is your ability to stack acts of leadership on top of each other, day in and day out. If you do this and you focus on the process, they add up to big wins and big influence.

Push for a purpose

Dee Ann Turner, a lifelong employee at Chick-fil-A and author of *It's My Pleasure* taught me a lot about how critical the purpose of Chick-fil-A's business is to its success.

Chick-fil-A was going through their first sales slump ever in the 1980's and Truett Cathy, the founder, had just made some big financial investments in real estate and at the corporate headquarters. Cathy announced the executive management team would be having a weekend retreat to figure out what the company was going to do about this sales slump. Many of the corporate employees thought the worst and figured the executive management team would come back from their retreat with a round of layoffs. Instead what happened changed the trajectory of the company for the next 40 years. The team came back with a purpose statement:

"To glorify God by being a faithful steward of all that is entrusted to us and to have a positive influence on all who come into contact with Chick-fil-A."

This purpose statement has remained the same for 40 years and is displayed outside of their corporate office in Atlanta for every single employee to see each day. Ever since the corporate executive retreat, Chick-fil-A has never looked back in terms of having more fulfilled employees and revenue growth.

It's not hard to understand people are more fulfilled, engaged, and perform better at work when there is a strong business purpose. You might not be in a position to create or change the purpose of your organization, but you can influence upper management to establish one or to better communicate it. There are many ways to go about this, but simply starting the conversation by asking questions of organizational leaders what the purpose of the business is can be a great way to start.

As you reflect on these concepts and begin thinking about incorporating them into your life here is an exercise you can do. Rate each of the 5 concepts in order of importance to you. Here is an example:

1. Don't forget the meaning of leadership
2. Have a sense of urgency
3. Control what you can control
4. Get small wins daily
5. Push for purpose

Then take the list and figure out how you are going to put each one into practice one day at a time. In the example above, if I were trying not to forget the meaning of leadership, I would write it down on the white board in my office so I can see it everyday. If it's, "control what you can control" write down E + R = O and the next event that happens, then put it through the equation. If it's having a sense of urgency, set your alarm for 5:30AM tomorrow. You get the point. These do absolutely no good without putting them into action and the only thing holding them back from action is your habits.

You don't need permission to lead, instead, you have the power to choose to lead. So carry leadership over and pass it onto others because we need more leaders, not less.

13

Purposeful Dreamers

"All men dream: but not equally. Those who dream by night in the dusty recesses of their minds wake up in the day to find it was vanity, but the dreamers of the day are dangerous men, for they may act their dreams with open eyes, to make it possible." - T.E. LAWRENCE

In today's modern world there is absolutely no telling what the future holds. Some of the latest research on workforce automation and computers reveals as many as 47% of jobs in the US are at risk of computerization (Oxford University)

Millions of jobs will be replaced by technology, leaving millions of people to develop new skills, create new industries and develop new jobs. Many jobs or job titles might not even exist today that people will have in 5, 10 or 20 years. Take this question as an example. When do you think the title Chief Executive Office (CEO) first started being used? 1800, 1850, 1900? Wrong on all accounts. The term CEO didn't even exist until after WWII. Think about that. All those who dreamed about having a certain job title prior to the 1940's couldn't even have dreamed of being a CEO because the title didn't exist. Now think about the speed our businesses run at today. There is a high likelihood the job or role of your dream doesn't even exist yet.

Why Dreaming is Still Important

The American Dream is supposed to be the standard for not only those in America but for people all around the world. The one your parents, grandparents or teachers have taught you about. The one that was made famous by James Truslow Adams in 1931 when he wrote," that dream is a land in which life should be better and richer and fuller for everyone, with the opportunity for each according to ability or achievement." As you get older it seems prophetic, which is why so many in prior generations fell in love with his dream. But somewhere along the road, Adams' dream faded. Maybe it was decades of prosperity in America that caused complacency, maybe it was the brokenness in homes or maybe it was that people just got lazy. In many ways it doesn't matter why it faded, the point is it did. It has caused a generation to struggle to understand why they exist and what they are meant to do. It's caused the highest job hopping rates of all time, limited innovation, a disengaged workforce and a bunch of individuals looking out for their own self-interests instead of the greater good of all.

Instead of trying to recreate the American Dream or resurrecting it from whatever graveyard it's in, the time has come for you to dream. Without a dream it will be extremely difficult to be a leader. Robert Kennedy famously said, "There are those who look at things the way they are, and ask why? I dream of things that never were and ask why not?."

I had the great fortune of interviewing Bill McDermott, the CEO of SAP, who wrote a book called, *"Winner's Dream."* In his book, Bill so eloquently said "We are all entitled to a dream and when you believe strongly enough in the dream, no one can take that away from you."

Senator Kennedy and Bill McDermott couldn't be more correct. This world needs people like you to dream big, with one simple caveat: you can't get in the way of others.

Your dream can't be one where there is only one winner. It can't be about stepping on others to realize your dream. If I've learned one thing, it is that nothing great happens alone. Unfortunately we have too many modern professionals sitting on the sidelines either living out someone else's dream or worse, not having one at all.

The majority of almost every generation is living for the weekend. It's gotten so bad, that people get into work on Monday morning and they are planning their Friday night before they have thought about work. It's as if this modern generation has been split into three distinct categories.

- Weekend Dreamers
- Financial Dreamers
- Purposeful Dreamers

Weekend Dreamers

I estimate Weekend Dreamers makeup about 50% of the millennial generation. They don't necessarily like the work they do, it's just a job they do to pay the bills and many times they feel trapped or suffocated by their job. They show up on Monday and can't wait for the clock to hit 5:30PM. They love taking breaks, rarely care about how successful they are in their job and are floating through life without much care for what's going on around them. The weekend dreamers aren't measuring success or are future-focused at all. Instead they're worried more about instant gratification and giving into their every urge.

Financial Dreamers

Financial Dreamers make up about 40% of the millennial generation. They have solely monetary purpose and are out working their tail off to either provide a better life for themselves and their family or to get themselves to the next financial class. The reasons vary; many times it's out of necessity because they didn't grow up with much and they don't want that life ever again. Others just want more. Once they get the taste of financial success, there isn't much that can stand in the way of the next vacation, car, house, or status symbol . They measure success based on the material possessions they own.

Purposeful Dreamers

I estimate Purposeful Dreams to be the remaining 10% of the current millennial generation. They have a purpose for being on earth, they know why they are here, they can clearly communicate it and they act on it. They are thoughtful about how their actions impact those around them and they dream bigger than themselves.

The factors are endless in what causes young people to fall into these three categories. The popular answers are: socioeconomic upbringing, genes, family life, organizational culture, friendship circles, mentors, teachers, schools or universities. While I don't have the answer, my best guess is it's a combination of everything listed because people are impacted or influenced at different times in their lives. Since I don't think we will ever have a scientific answer, let's focus on why it's important more people become purposeful with their dreams. Purposeful dreamers have full lives, love going to work, love going home and love life. This doesn't mean 100% of the time they love all of these areas, but the majority of the time they are fulfilled and happy.

How Dreams Become a Reality

I have learned many things in my life but maybe none more than the fact that everything rises and falls based on leadership. Your ability to get others to help make your dream become a reality isn't possible without leadership. So whether you are an entry-level employee with a dream of becoming the CEO or an entrepreneur with a grand dream to solve world poverty, the common element will be your ability to get others to help make your dream become a reality. If you don't have that kind of clarity of purpose about your professional journey, think back to our example of the infiltration of technology and workforce automation. The one area that workforce automation and computers can't replace are leaders. Leadership is the one element that will make a major difference in your life both at work and at home. Being a leader is worth following, makes life rich and it's my hope you will make the choice to be a purposeful dreamer. This is one who will act on their dreams in the face of uncertainty and long odds and understand that your professional career is a journey.

Imagine if every professional started their professional journey with the framework of F.M.L. as the foundation of which to add value to their organization and the world? Wouldn't the relationships and impact that people can have on the world be better by implementing F.M.L.?: Following First, then focusing on their Development, and lastly Leading by example?

1. **F - Follow First**. Before you can effectively lead, you must learn to follow.

2. **M - My Development.** Being a lifelong learner is essential to personal and professional growth. Focusing on you own personal development goes a long way in becoming the best version of yourself you can be.

3. **L - Lead By Example**. You communicate your ability to lead through your actions. The best way to lead no matter where you are in your career   is by example.

I believe in my core it would. My hope is the F.M.L. framework will be a set of best practices and ideas to help you move up and lead by example. If this book inspired you, please pass it along to others whose life may be impacted by it as well.

Notes

The purpose of the Follow My Lead Podcast is to transfer stories of today's leaders to the leaders of tomorrow. The show has 50+ episodes with guests like; SAP CEO Bill McDermott, Sealed Air CEO Jerome Peribere, Dale Partridge, Dee Ann Turner, Tom Ziglar, Jon Gordon and Bob Beaudine.

To listen to the podcast just search, "Follow My Lead" wherever you listen to podcasts or go to learnloft.com/podcast.

What our listeners are saying:

"WOW. This is an awesome podcast. There is so much to learn every week." Connie

"What a great find. John delivers important messages to professionals from all ages. He really understand the current leadership landscape." - Ryan

"This podcast changed my life." - Carrie

"Great show! I am a big fan, John always has fascinating content and brilliant guests. I can't recommend it enough" - Sandra

John Eades is the founder of LearnLoft and host of the
Follow My Lead Podcast. He is passionate about the
development of people. He writes and speaks about
Leadership Development and Organizational Alignment to
the Modern Professional. His articles have been featured in
LinkedIn Pulse, Training Industry Magazine, and eLearning
Industry. John resides in Charlotte, NC with his wife Amy
and two children, John Ellis and Lucy.

You can follow and connect with John on social media on
Facebook, Instagram and Twitter @johngeades. Seriously,
let him know what you thought of the book.

Made in the USA
Middletown, DE
17 February 2017